GARAGE SALE
America

GARAGE SALE
America

BRUCE LITTLEFIELD

COLLINS DESIGN

An Imprint of HarperCollinsPublishers

Garage Sale America
Copyright © 2007 by Bruce Littlefield

HarperCollins books may be purchased for educational, business, or sales promotional use. For information, please write: Special Markets Department, HarperCollins Publishers, 10 East 53rd Street, New York, NY 10022.

First Edition

First published in 2007 by:
Collins Design,
An Imprint of HarperCollins*Publishers*
10 East 53rd Street
New York, NY 10022
Tel: (212) 207-7000
Fax: (212) 207-7654
collinsdesign@harpercollins.com
www.harpercollins.com

Distributed throughout the world by:
HarperCollins*Publishers*
10 East 53rd Street
New York, NY 10022
Fax: (212) 207-7654

Design by Kay Schuckhart/Blond on Pond

Library of Congress Cataloging-in-Publication Data

Littlefield, Bruce (Bruce Duanne)
  Garage sale America / Bruce Littlefield. -- 1st ed.
    p. cm.
  ISBN-13: 978-0-06-115165-1 (pbk.)
  ISBN-10: 0-06-115165-3 (pbk.)
1. Garage sales--United States. I. Title.

HF5482.3.L58 2007
381'.1950973--dc22

                                        2006101335

Printed in China
First Printing, 2007

For my grandmother, Winifred Bruce, who taught me how to hunt

C O N T E N T S

New! Pyrex Bowls
in the colors of
Spring Flowers
...only $250

INTRODUCTION

Sale Today!

Garage sale. Yard sale. Tag sale. Barn sale. Rummage sale. Estate sale. Stoop sale. Call it what you want sale, it describes one thing—the best deal in America. Fun, generally tax free, and useful, nothing beats a garage sale transaction. It's the happiest of all star-spangled exchanges: "I want what you don't want, but how much don't you want it for?" There's just something neighborly about being invited into someone's yard or home and encouraged to paw through their stuff. And allowed to buy it or pass judgment on it.

A HUNTING WE WILL GO

Yes, each Saturday morning around the country (and in warm weather most other days, too) anthropological voyeuristic warriors pour themselves ther-

moses of coffee, grab their maps, circled newspapers, and fistfuls of dollars, and set out for an archeological dig through the soils of pop culture. They know the day may bring the discovery of an underpriced hundred-year-old handmade quilt right down table from an overpriced pile of Beanie Babies.

Garage sale hunters like me don't head out to the sale saying we need a vintage sprinkler or a Red Riding Hood cookie jar. Rather, we head out hunting for just the thing we've always wanted, even though we don't know exactly what that is. But when we spot it we know we need it, we have to have it, and by Melmac! we're going to buy it.

"I collect costume jewelry," one delightful southern woman told me as she carefully picked through a hap-hazardly jumbled mélange of vintage trinkets in an old shoebox. "I'm in the business. I have a website: dubya, dubya, dubya dot beadifulworld dot bizzZZZ. I also collect salt and pepper shakers." She smiled, nodded, and dove back into the shoebox.

SAVE THE DATE
National Garage Sale Day:
Second Saturday in August.
Started by Dan Rhodes,
Hoover, Alabama.

TRASH OR TREASURE?

It is at times a strange dichotomy—trash to one, treasure to another—but what people are drawn to at garage sales is ultimately a study of what makes us tick. "My mother had one of those" is thrown around quite

To Protect and Serve

HIGHWAY PATROL

POLICE 287

Early birds will be shot.

–Sign outside a garage sale in Pennsylvania

often on the hunt and can mean either I want it and can't live without it or I wouldn't take that off this table if you paid me, depending on just how fond those childhood memories are. Many garage sale purchases are sentimental: we see things that  remind us of a pleasant moment or a time from our past. Nostalgia is certainly part of the hook for both buyer and seller. The seller is selling it because said item no longer needs to be a part of her life and the buyer is buying it because it has to be a part of his. Other purchases are practical, useful for our workaday present: a fully loaded toolbox, for example. There are real treasures to be found if you know how to spot them and are able to think outside the mall.

The thrill of the hunt is finding that needle in the haystack, the nugget of gold amidst the coal, the missing butter dish to my Grandma's 1954 Franciscan Starburst dinnerware. And finding it before some other seamstress, gold digger, or grandson lays his hands on it. There's nothing more thrilling than reeling in something cheap that is perfect for our needs. Whether refrigerator big or marble small, I've seen and bought it all, and figured out how to get it home.

I suppose, looking back, it was my grandmother who got me addicted to the thrill of the hunt. Most Saturdays of my childhood, she'd tote me around to yard sales in the small mill town of Enoree, South Carolina, where we'd talk to friends old and new and poke through their stuff. My grandmother would give me a quarter or two to pick out something special, and I'd pore over the decision of how to spend my coins as if it were the most important decision of my life.

I didn't buy the normal kids' things.

I'd buy an old bottle so I could cut snapdragons for the center of our Sunday dinner table, a bolt of red cloth to tie giant ribbons around the pecan trees for Christmas, and once, when I was really lucky, I found an autographed photo of Carol Burnett from the preacher's neighbor's sale. (Yes, I realize now that the seller may have signed it herself, but at the time it was as if Carol had sent it to me personally.) *Carol, is that you?*

CHEAP CHIC

Today, the joy of decorating with garage sale finds gives me the same satisfaction. In fact, I've had amazing fun and great success decorating in vintage garage sale items. Gorgeous, inexpensive, and easy. It's imperfectly perfect—cheap chic.

With every new purchase, I'm buying things that make me happy and make my home feel comfortable.

There's no "Get your feet off that coffee table!" in my house as was the case in my father's. My coffee table is a 1904 Lipton Coffee shipping box I got for $5 from the basement of an estate sale and you're welcome to put your feet on it. I have it filled with toys and party games so when kids come over (or my cocktail friends) I can quickly lay my hands on some fun.

More fastidious types hit sales armed with the measurements of every nook and cranny in their house, accompanied by a specific list of needs for, say, their bathroom renovation. However practical,

TAKE A LOOK AT SALES IN . . . *Florida* if you want treasures like high-end glass, Tiffany lamps, and sterling silver. Florida is filled with retirees and lifetimes of accumulated junk. The best places to shop are in the ritzy neighborhoods along the coasts.

more often than not, I've just seen it as a setup for disappointment. There are only so many claw-foot tubs that have been extracted from bathrooms and toted to the lawn, and there is a high probability that I'll need to take a bath before I happen upon one at a sale. So, if I'm looking for something large and specific, and need it sooner rather than later, I check out my local salvage yard/junkshop where someone else will have scoured for years in order to amass a collection of tubs in all shapes, colors, and sizes. I have, however, been known to buy something special when I've seen it—like my early barber's pole—and then plan a project around it. And I do have some antique juggling balls that I bought a few years back, promising myself to learn.

THE ONE THAT GOT AWAY

There's nothing worse than the one that got away. It haunts you for weeks like a bad dream, eats away at your psyche like a termite on softened wood. I recently found myself attracted to a delicately aged pair of Bert and Ernie puppets sitting on the lawn of an otherwise innocuous sale of miscellany. My brother and I had them growing up. Ernie slept on the bottom bunk with Brian; Bert slept up top with me. I didn't buy them, leaving them to be taken by some other more thoughtful brother, and I've regretted it ever since. It would have been fun for me to send Brian an Ernie with a mysterious note—definitely worth the ten bucks. It was a real missed opportunity, and I try not to let those happen too often.

Letting a find get away is simply not an option for many people. I've seen women pounce on a vase like two cats going after the same mouse, then hiss at

Garage Sale 101

- Arrows and directions should be clear, easy to read, and accurate.
- Greeting people is common human courtesy.
- Bring cash. Have change.
- A clean item sells for more than a dirty one.
- Expect to negotiate.
- Honesty is the best policy.
- Don't steal.
- Don't say "it's real" when you know it's not.
- Dangerous things should be labeled as such and kept out of reach of children.
- Obey the law.

each other until one backs down. I've watched grown men fondle vintage tools in the middle of the pouring rain as lightning struck around them, the ultimate standoff in order to scoop up a coveted hacksaw. I myself have been known to tromp through the snow in the dead of winter for a rare off-season sale and been happy about it even when I only bagged a 25¢ stuffed animal for my dog.

BRAGGING RIGHTS

Garage saling is a hope-based adventure—a modern-day gold rush. We can't wait to brag about the bargain we got on a mid-century lamp or the $5 we paid for an entire set of Bakelite flatware. Even if we come back empty-handed, we have great stories of junk, of oddities so freakish they belong in a sideshow, and of people and their varying tastes and proclivities.

From little towns in South Carolina to Santa Monica, from South Beach to a rural village in New

The Junk Kings
Stan and Gary Zaborski

Stan Zaborski, Stanthejunkman.com, of Zaborski Emporium; "If I don't have it, I probably know somebody that does."

For something as specific as a pair of antique French doors or authentic pedestal sink, I seek professional help: garage salers who indeed buy the entire garage. They are a snappish bunch, known as architectural salvage experts or, more commonly, junk dealers. Two of my favorites are Gary and Stan Zaborski, infamous dueling brothers of junk in Kingston, New York.

Local legend has it that years ago the brothers had a tiff over a toy train set and never spoke again. But neither of them talks about it. Gary kept Stan'z, the business that their father, Stan Zaborski, Sr., started in 1962. Stan moved his treasures into an old shirt factory; his shop is called Zaborski Emporium.

I met Gary at Stan'z when he sold me a pair of French doors for a song. After an ordeal of getting them home tied to the roof, I toted them to where they would soon be installed "for appreciation value." It was only then that I noticed the slight problem. I didn't have a pair of French doors, I had a French door and a French door from opposite sides of France.

I loaded the mismatched pair back onto the roof and headed back to Kingston. I found Gary standing beside a lion cage. I approached sheepishly. "I have a problem . . ." I began in my most pitiful tone.

"What's up?" he asked.

"Well, the pair of French doors I bought isn't a pair after all."

"You can't make them work?" he urged.

"Only if I decide to go for that funhouse look," I laughed.

"Okay, bring 'em in," he agreed. I leaned the doors against an old streetlamp, and he handed back my cash.

As I was leaving, I spotted eight bungalow chairs perfect for my dining room table. "Just got those in," Gary said. "Hundred bucks for all eight."

"Sold," I said. "I'll pick them up later."

Then, I drove over to Stan's where, among his three thousand doors, I finally found the matching pair I needed.

Gary Zaborski of Stan'z: "That's priced like I really don't want to sell it."

Hampshire, I've seen, stopped at, and bought things at every kind of sale in America. I've been to sales in churches so primitive they didn't have plumbing, and in barns so big maps were provided. I've found big loot in small towns and gold cuff links on a stoop in Brooklyn. I've met dog walkers turned garage sale performance artists and a nuclear power plant operator turned yard sale queen. I've met the oldest seller and the youngest. And, of course, I've met my neighbors in their own backyards.

Yard hopping, garage stopping, and barn storming provide free tours of pop culture and American lives without admission fees. These activities are the ultimate reality television in which you co-star with people who will tell you everything you need to know about their lives. Yes, garage saling is the mecca of voyeurism, and you, as the nosy Gladys Kravitz, don't have to hide behind the drapes or peer between the cracks of the fence. You can snoop, poke, and peek right out in the open. There's no need for secretiveness, proven by the fact that I've personally witnessed people put their underwear drawers out on the lawn and provide narration as you burrow around in them. "Those were my ex-husband's," one seller told me as I poked in a pile of matchbooks. "If you want 'em, you can have 'em all for a quarter."

TAKE A LOOK AT SALES IN . . . *California* if you would like to find entertainment memorabilia. Forget Beverly Hills; although it's very affluent, its laws are strict on yard sales. Instead, check out the trendy Silver Lake area where lots of writers and producers live. If you're looking for mid-century modern furniture head over to Palm Springs, where all the Alexander homes were built in the fifties.

Finding out about ex-husbands, feuding neighbors, and unwelcome tagalong mothers-in-law is par for the course, as is making fast acquaintance with those who sell you their castoffs. You do, after all, now share something in common: you now own their great grandma's china that she got as a wedding gift.

Besides their penchants and secrets, garage salers are also generally willing to tell all they know about everything from fishing lures to Swanky Swigs and will be happy to help you figure out a way to get the goods off their property. I've had deliveries of everything from a fifties-era medical cabinet to giant

barn doors. That kind of hospitable friendliness keeps garage salers coming back for more.

SECRETS

Yes, we garage sale in droves. Every fifteen seconds in the United States a garage saler puts out his arrowed sign, and conservative numbers put lookers, pickers, and choosers making around five hundred million stop-and-shops a year. The mostly off-the-book industry is estimated to be around $3 billion a year, but *shhh*, let's keep that our little secret.

This is, in fact, a book of secrets. You'll learn how to spot a treasure, how to steal a deal, and how to develop a unique decorating style incorporating garage sale finds. But this adventure is more than that. It is also a celebration of American life, a scrapbook of our treasures and of what makes us happy.

Garage saling crosses all economic, political, and religious lines. You can love an old Howdy Doody doll whether you live in a red or blue state. Spend five minutes at any garage sale, and you'll discover happiness from people on both sides of the table. It's something we all have in common—the love of a good bargain, the discovery of something new, the reclaiming of something old. We can talk about these things with pure delight. Garage saling is something that unites us.

How could you not fall in love with garage saling? It's

perfect entertainment: fascinating characters, long-lost treasures, decorating choices, and true stories that are often stranger than fiction. Saling is the perfect antidepressant because it's a good deal for all involved. The experience of finding just the right thing for just the right price is emotionally rewarding, economically clever, and environmentally sound.

There are many things we would throw away if we were not afraid others might pick them up.

– *Oscar Wilde,* The Picture of Dorian Gray *(1891)*

A TABLE FULL OF STORIES

The stories here are, at surface, of the pursuit of objects we adore, but as people talk about those objects—whether with fondness or good-riddance—we get a vivid snapshot of the life of the beholder. Looking at a garage sale—its objects and its citizens—is like visiting an art gallery filled with detailed self-portraits.

This is a fascinating journey—a search for treasures and ourselves—looking over the shoulder of some fabulous characters and looking back at some of our favorite things, one garage sale at a time.

Let's go saling. What is it *you're* looking for?

PART I

ADVENTURE

Treasure-Hunting Fever

Sales can be called many things. In the city, I've been to a lobby sale where I watched a man score an Eames desk and chair for fifty bucks. In the south, I've been to an old plantation porch sale where I scored a mint julep for free and an antique quilt for $10. Off Melrose Avenue in Los Angeles, I've been to a sidewalk sale where I saw a woman walk off with an armload of vintage designer purses for $25. And on a rainy day tent sale in Seattle I found a vintage replica of the Space Needle for $2. The possibilities are limitless and the pursuit contagious.

BARN SALE: THE BEST ONE EVER

When my gardener friend Mary Cleary told me she was going to have a barn sale, I knew two things: it was going to be big, and I was going to get lucky.

I knew Mary's sale would be grade A. She's been collecting stuff in that barn of hers since she and her husband Tim sold their Minnesota dairy farm and moved to the Catskills ten years ago. Mary has an eye for fabulous things, a penchant for buying, and the barn to put the overflow in. "Do you think having it on the Saturday of Memorial Day weekend would be okay?" she asked, as she helped me plant my shade garden.

"No," I said, digging my shovel into the dirt. "You have to start your sale on Friday morning, that way you'll get the dealers."

"I really don't think people will come," Mary doubted, her blue-gloved hands covered in compost. "Nobody will want our junk."

"First of all, it's not junk, Mary," I instructed. "It's 'treasures.' Second of all, you're obviously going to need help pricing." I volunteered. *That way*, I strategically schemed, *I'll be the first in line.*

Barn sales have become a personal favorite. There are only a handful of these preeminent sales a year, although some people call their events barn sales while featuring "unopened Pokemon cards," old VHS tapes, and a hodgepodge of mismatched coffee mugs—not exactly the real McCoy.

At a great summertime barn sale you can find big pieces—chairs, gates, and farmhouse kitchen sinks—as well as an array of tools, signs, jars, and most anything else. When I first bought a house in upstate New York, I discovered the joy of the barn sale right down the street at the Kern Farm. I got many treasures at Fred Bell's great yearly sale, including an old Victrola with almost a hundred turn-of-the-century records and a pair of hundred-year-old gates.

My favorite barn seller is Kent Korber of Alligerville, New York. His wares are always crowd-pleasers. When he posts his notice, I'll reschedule an emergency appendectomy around it. Besides perfect signage (time, dates, location, and removal of signs after the sale), Kent sends out an e-mail announcing his extravaganza and invites his past big spenders (me) to a continental breakfast at 7:30 A.M. He's got it down.

While we big spenders munch on our muffins, we have a clear view from Kent's kitchen of the tarp-covered tables by his barn; this really cranks up the adrenaline. Though the conversation is polite, the strategizing is evident. Each year, as I sip my coffee I plan my route around the site, and around others like Sue from the Barking Dog, who is always certain to go for exactly what I want. Even though she's probably eighty, that girl can run.

If you've ever seen that game on *Price is Right* where contestants run back

and forth trying to match price tags to potential prizes and pulling the lever to see how many they got right, you've seen the chaos that is the opening of a sale. Last year I planned to first take a bench, followed by an urn and plant stand, which I'd place on the bench off to the side to indicate my "claim," then I'd dash into the barn for "smalls," hopefully some vintage Christmas ornaments. By the 8:00 A.M. opening there is always a hopeful crowd gathered, some of us

hungrier than others because we'd been in Kent's kitchen drooling over the tarps while eating our breakfast.

When Kent dropped the rope, everyone lunged forward like racehorses out of the gate. You wouldn't believe the mad dash. While I was successfully nabbing the bench, Sue grabbed the plant stand and a woman I didn't know grabbed my urn. I did, however, walk away a winner in the smalls category, scoring an aluminum Christmas tree for my ever-growing collection.

MARY'S BARN SALE

As Mary's barn sale approached, my anticipation grew like a weed in May. I acted as her advisor and confidant during the all-important pre-event organizing, giving her signage and pricing tips, as well as reassuring her that she had lots of desirable loot.

When the big weekend finally arrived, here's how it unfolded:

6:00 A.M. Friday morning, clear skies. My alarm clock buzzed, announcing that the sale of the century had finally arrived. I jumped out of bed, threw on clothes, and staggered out to the car.

6:25 A.M. Farm Stand. Coffee.

6:45 A.M. County Route 6. I watched Tim zoom around a curve in his truck, obviously on a sign-hanging mission. I honked and waved.

6:55 A.M. After passing a perfectly painted sign heralding their address, dates, and times at the start of their road, I rumbled down Mary and Tim's driveway, past the cedar fence, and parked beside the majesty of Mary's blooming garden. Mary was by the barn, and I could tell she was angry.

"I'm so mad at Tim I can't stand it," Mary seethed. "I know he threw the bag with my price tags in it into the fire." Mary had cleverly gotten garage sale price tags—10¢, 25¢, up to $20, and even Make Offer, all on round, neon-colored stickers—which she'd shown me the day before during our signage discussion.

"They're here somewhere," I said.

"He throws everything into that damn fire," Mary grumbled, dumping a box of pulleys onto a table. "How much do you think for these?"

"Sell 'em as a set," I decided, putting them back into the box. "We should hurry, Mary, people will be here soon."

"It starts at nine," Mary said as she fretted about looking for her neon-colored stickers. "We have two hours." I took a moment to explain to Mary that no matter what the sign says, once it's up the sale is fair game. As I finished my explanation, a blue minivan with I BUY POSTCARDS painted on the side zoomed down the driveway.

7:20 A.M. Before we could say "twenty-five cents," the barn sale had begun.

By 8:00 A.M. Mary had found the price tags (she'd left them behind the barn), Tim had forgiven Mary's incendiary "pyromaniac" accusations, I'd spent $273, and Mary and Tim's 9:00 A.M. barn sale had a crowd.

8:55 A.M. Out of money and late for a meeting, I rolled down the window and gave Mary my parting words of advice: "Now if somebody asks if you can do better, say, 'It's the first day of the sale, why don't you check back on Sunday—everything will be half price.' Either they'll take it then, or they'll be back." She leaned in the car, kissed me, and I backed up the driveway past a flock of incoming bargain hunters.

Throughout the day, my hourly calls to Mary's cell phone were greeted with "Can't talk, got a crowd," or "There are so many people here, I'll call you back," or "That'll be twenty-two dollars." I knew it was going well.

Saturday. I made my way over to the barn sale that had become an all-out party. Mack and Yvonne, Mary and Tim's neighbors, were using things from the sale—a giant hat, a cane, and some Christmas tinsel—to revive their old borscht belt act. Tim was giving guided tours of the massive log house they built entirely themselves. And Mary, between sales, was teaching an inquisitive group of "weekenders" about deer-resistant plants. I happily found another carload of treasures in Mary's second-day unveilings, including a painting titled *The End Was Seen by the Kool-Aid Queen.*

Sunday. Mary and Tim's sale became a "Take what you want giveaway."

"You know that dresser?" Mary whispered, as she began the end-of-sale report, "That went for five dollars."

"*Five dollars!*" I screamed. "That was priced at *fifty* dollars."

"Yeah," Mary giggled, "But we discovered it had been mothballed and varnished over—it sort of stunk." The girl who bought it was thrilled, especially when Tim offered to deliver it after watching her try to ram it into her Toyota's trunk. Mary had even been shocked at that one. "You're going to deliver a five-dollar dresser?" she asked her husband of forty years.

"Five dollars!" he said, dropping his jaw. "The last time I looked that dresser was fifty dollars."

"Everything's on sale today," Mary reminded him.

Mary's favorite gang was a bunch of punk kids with lots of piercings. One of the girls asked her friend for a quarter in order to buy six books for $1. "Honey," Mary grinned in a state of barn sale bliss, "For you, they are six for seventy-five cents."

Dan, Mary's son, had brought to the sale a pile of hip designer clothes from his modeling days that he was giving away for a quarter each. "That outfit has danced at every club in Manhattan," Dan told one teenage boy who was dreamily looking at the clothes. Dan heaped the entire pile into the kid's arms and said: "Have fun!" The kid did a jig of excitement.

Before the group of kids left, Mary grabbed a pink hat and plopped it on top of a girl's head. "Here," Mary smiled triumphantly. "You have to have this—it matches your hair."

The barn sale was a roaring success. Lots of people got lots of treasures and Mary and Tim proved that when you give, you can also receive.

GARAGE SALE: ONE IS NOT LIKE EVERY OTHER

When you've seen one garage sale you haven't seen them all. You'll find something for your living room at one, a missing piece to your china at another, and it's likely you'll discover something completely new before the end of the day that will become an obsession for the future. It is this ever-changing amalgam that keeps us salers coming back for more, and why I've found myself waking at unnatural hours in order to plunder through someone else's discards for most of my adult life.

Take down your signs, people! We salers are making a pact. If signs are left up, your home is fair game. This means we can knock on your door shortly after sunrise, rifle through your stuff, and demand a discount.

One snowy winter, for example, a fresh dusting of snow was on the ground when in a move only an addict would make, I rolled out of bed and jumped in the car in order to be the first to arrive at the season's one and only moving sale. I had seen the sign announcing the momentous event in a fleeting drive-by the day before and spent most of the night dreaming about the treasures I was sure the earliest sale of the year would hold.

Moving sales are hit or miss, since some bewildering people want to tote the treasures with them when they move and leave their junk behind. My hope was that these "moving outers" were definitely going to want to unload all their heavy Pyrex and cumbersome antique clutter, and, of course, they wouldn't want to drag that old weathered leather club chair to a new house.

In my off-season desperation, I overlooked the obvious: No one moves in the dead of winter and has a sale. It defies natural order. But when you're jonesing, you'll believe anything, including a sign that was left behind months before. In spite of the obvious, I pathetically drove up and down the road for thirty minutes, hoping beyond growing suspicion that these moving outers were still here and just late in setting up. They weren't. They had moved on. Months ago. And left their sign up to rot. Unfortunately, contrary to some sellers' beliefs, these signs do not take themselves down. In fact, they have a half-life almost as long as nuclear waste, and are as annoying as a paper cut.

Take down your signs, people! We salers are making a pact. If signs are left up, your home is fair game. This means we can knock on your door shortly after sunrise, rifle through your stuff, and demand a discount.

But signs are just the beginning. Sales come by many different names, with varying merchandise, fluctuating prices, and, of course, diverse setups. I've come to know a few things about sales after years of observation and obsession, and I've come to a few conclusions:

Garage Sale is a typically generic term—and has come to be a universal code for: I'm selling my stuff, and I'm selling it cheap. Often the hosts do

indeed have a garage. Sometimes they even sell out of it. Items can range from things the seller is too lazy to take to the dump to family heirlooms they no longer cherish. On the low end are dregs such as three floral saucers without cups, a Hot Mama license-tag holder, and a half-used tube of Neosporin. But often, amidst the household clutter, an I-can't-believe-they're-getting-rid-of-that moment will occur. During high hunting season, a morning without such an incident is rare.

At a sale last fall, for example, I was casually scanning a drop cloth covered in junk, when, sitting like a jewel on a giant pile of dung, I eyed the matching platter to my set of heirloom Franciscan Starburst dishes. I eased my way to it, and lifted it from a stack of old towels. No chips, no flakes, no grazing. Whirling around to ask the all-important question, I knocked a grouping of tennis cans off a makeshift sawhorse table.

"How much?" I asked, as tennis balls volleyed about the driveway.

"Hey, Randy!" the Hostess screamed from her PVC chaise lounger. "How much you want for your balls?"

"Three dollars!" the tubby former tennis player garbled back through a mouthful of Snickers.

"No," I replied calmly, my insides shivering with excitement. "I mean the platter."

"Oh *that*?" the Hostess sneered, wrinkling her nose in disgust. "That's a quarter. There's a matching casserole dish somewhere. That's a quarter, too."

Moments like that make it all worthwhile.

The Trachtenburg Family Slideshow Players Jason, Tina, and Rachel

The Trachtenburg family found their life's calling at a garage sale. While running a successful dog-walking service, The Dog Squad, in Seattle, they had the opportunity to make garage sales and estate sales a part of their daily reality. "We were walking literally thousands of dogs in the fancier neighborhoods where they sell all the good stuff," Jason, the father of the family, remembers. "Up until then, I was playing a lot of open mic nights, but my music wasn't clicking with the audience. I had no momentum."

One day, when his wife Tina was walking a dog, she stumbled into a sale where she bought a slide projector for $5 and a box of slides for a quarter. The slide projector sat in the closet for a month or so until one night Jason pulled it out and said, "Let's turn it on and see if it works." Fortunately, the bulb was working or all else might be different today. What they watched was a slideshow titled Trip to Japan, 1959, that told in pictures the story of a husband and wife taking a vacation to Japan. "Pretty simple," Jason admits, "But it was a hook."

Organically the song "Mountain Trip to Japan, 1959" spilled out of Jason, and he started performing it at the end of his regular set. It went over like lemonade on a hot summer day, and the family—Tina on slides, six-year-old Rachel on drums, Jason on keyboards and guitar—dressed in Tina's garage-sale-inspired creations and entered a talent contest. They won the first prize of $500, and the Trachtenburg Family Slideshow Players, a post-modern, indie-pop-rock Partridge Family, was hatched.

Since that time, they've gained an international cult following, both for their music and their garage sale sensibilities. "It worked within our economic means," Jason says of their novel repurposing. "And came directly from our garage sale lifestyle. By acquiring our slides, our clothes, our bric-a-brac from other people's unwanted castoffs, it's the least environmental impact we can have. If we can make art out of the excesses of our overwhelming culture, then that is highly evolved."

YARD SALE: DRAGGING IT TO THE LAWN

Yard sales, like garage sales, sell household castoffs, but from tarps and makeshift tables spread around the lawn and driveway of the house. I've found these sales provide a certain convenience for the buyer, like a drive-through window. With everything splayed out on the lawn, it is often easy to

decide thumbs up or thumbs down with a slow drive-by. Though admittedly uncomfortable and rather embarrassing for the poor seller who, while sitting amidst her household trash, has to watch someone slowly drive past, gawk, then hit the gas, it sure saves time if you're out hunting.

Yard Saling 101 could be taught as a college course. I found a VHS tape starring Phyllis Diller, *How to Have a Moneymaking Garage Sale*, and, as you can imagine, she complains about husband Fang's excesses and how she makes a few bucks by cleaning out his closet.

One of my best yard sale finds is the show *Ida's Havin' a Yard Sale* written by and featuring the hilarious Susan Poulin. One afternoon, the impeccable storyteller treated me to a conversation with Ida LeClair, from Mahoosuc Mills, Maine, about everything from her budding knowledge of Feng Shui to crocheted toilet paper covers.

"I've learned through experience that having a successful yard sale is about marketing and product placement," said Ida. "You need something snappy in your ad to get folks' attention." Here's Ida's:

If you saw something you liked on the Home Shopping Network that you wished you'd bought but didn't, most likely I did, and I'll be selling it on Saturday. Yard sale 8:00–3:00. Collectibles, furniture, tools, all sorts of bargains. Early birds welcome.

"The Home Shopping Network is the hook," she explained. "That's what gets them to read more. Then you've got to say you have collectibles, because that's trendy. And if you don't think you have them, you do, because everything is collectible to someone. Haven't you seen the *Antiques Roadshow*?

"Furniture is important. You need a few big pieces to draw people in, make them stop and get out of their car. It's not worth your time to have a jelly jar yard sale. That's when there are a couple tables with lots of little trinkets on them. You'll just get drive-bys with those. If you don't have any furniture that you're ready to part with, just have your husband bring out a chest of drawers, a desk, a trunk, anything big. Then, put a few things on them that are for sale. People will stop to look at the furniture, and when they ask what the price is, you say, 'Oh, I'm sorry. That's not for sale. I'm just using that to display those collectibles.'

"Now, tools. I'm not big on them myself, but you need to put them in your ad for three reasons. Number one: it might get your husband to tidy up the shed. Number two: it keeps him occupied, so he's there when you need him to carry heavy things out to a car or truck. Number three: it's a code. It lets

you women know that there's going to be something at the yard sale to occupy your husband so you can really look around, and then he's there when you need him to lug stuff.

"You have to make sure your yard sale signs are fresh and new. You can make them by hand if you want, or use the ones that the newspaper gives you for taking out the ad. Just don't put up old ones. Then it looks like you're one of those places that's having a permanent yard sale. You've seen them: a house with lots of junk piled up in the yard all summer long; yard sale signs all weather-beaten because they've been out for years; blue tarps everywhere. I stopped at one once where they were trying to sell little packets of mustard and ketchup like you get at McDonald's. I mean, come on! Half used boxes of laundry detergent, and an old bedpan. Swear to God, an old bedpan!

"Why is it that the things you think are going to be snapped up in a flash don't sell? Meanwhile, the crap you almost put in the trash, meaning it wasn't even suitable for Good Will, is the first to go. For example, the first thing we sold today to the early birds was a set of beat up old Melmac dishes of Aunt Laura's. Meanwhile, the Precious Moments figurine with that little girl and boy kissing and their cute little poodle staring up at them . . . It's still here! Not even a nibble."

> **MELMAC**
> Melmac: Besides being a highly collectible brand name of dinnerware molded from the plastic melamine (also the main component of Formica), Melmac is the fictional home planet to the alien life form on the sitcom *ALF.*

TAKE A LOOK AT SALES IN . . . Connecticut's fancier neighborhoods to take advantage of "Robin Hood sales"—where taking from the rich can make anyone a Merry Man. Investment bankers collect lots of trendy, pricey furniture like Ethan Allen and Maurice Vilency that (to their tastes) have a short life span, and practically give their stuff away when they are done with it.

For Ida LeClair, yard sales are an opportunity to see how her unique creations
will move. "I always have a test-marketing table to see which items are most popular,
so we can make a bunch to sell before the Christmas Bazaar at St. Hyacinth's. This
year everything on the table was made out of shoulder pads we cut out of our
dresses, shirts, and sweaters. Couple of throw pillows decorated with shoulder pads,
shoulder pad potholders, trivets, a mobile for over the baby's crib, garlands. . . . My
personal favorite and our number-one seller was the shoulder pad wreath. It makes
a handsome decoration for the front door for the holidays. Non-denominational."

The Yard Sale Queen

History can't be bought at a mall. The Queen and her son, Jacob, with some of her found treasures. She says, "I love my trunk coffee table—it has authentic old stickers on the ends, New York to Paris, First Class Hold and Not Wanted on Voyage. If only it could talk."

Chris Heiska created the website Yardsalequeen.com, which provides a ton of helpful hints for yard salers, as well as her fun blog. She says of her yard sale life, "I used to be normal. I was working at the local nuclear power plant, and a friend there had created a website. She had so much fun doing it that I wanted to do it too. My husband said I should have a purpose, so I decided to put some tips out there on yard sales and see what happened. The response was crazy. It seems everyone can find something they love about yard saling.

"My first garage sale purchase was a troll doll when I was six or seven. I loved that thing. Growing up, my mom didn't garage sale, so after I got my driver's license I would stop at them on my own. When I got married we didn't have anything, so instead of sitting around in this big empty house, I went yard saling and found everything: furniture, art, and every last knickknack."

Like the rest of us saling fanatics, once she caught the bug there was no turning back. "I am now so addicted to yard sales that I even have dreams about going to them," Chris confesses. "I'm trying to cut down, but I'm an obsessive-compulsive shopper. My husband tolerates it, but the other day found my stash of ice cream scoopers hidden under the bed and asked 'Why does one woman need all those scoopers?' Everybody loves ice cream. Why not one for every flavor? There are all different designs, handles, and colors. Some are plastic; some are metal. I even have one with a wooden handle.

"My perfect day is a day without rain and a lot of sales, including some church sales, all evenly spaced apart in time, and each having exactly what I need. I've found everything at garage sales, even liquor! I've sworn off going to the mall—though I occasionally go to see the prices of things in the real world—because I generally find things that I have on my list at a yard sale; you're sort of drawn to it. Last week I needed stain for my son's swing set, and sure enough I found two gallons free at a sale. I don't know if the color is an exact match, but who cares, it didn't cost me a dime!"

TAG!: IN-THE-HOUSE SALES

In many parts of the country, Tag Sale has become a generic term like Garage Sale and Yard Sale; its meaning: come pay me to cart off my stuff. However, at traditional tag sales you're actually invited inside the house where you find everything, still in its natural habitat, tagged and ready to move. Besides getting to discover all kinds of houses, tag sales are a garage sale hunter's paradise with a wide range of finds.

I discovered the joys of the tag sale shortly after moving to Manhattan when, in an attempt to combine getting off the island with garage sale shopping, I rented a car and drove north, through the Bronx and up to Stamford, Connecticut.

It was an early Saturday morning and there were several garage sale signs posted along the route, but they were in the minority. Tag sale was the sign du jour, and though I was at the time unfamiliar with the semantics, their offerings were enticing. "Furniture!" "1960s." "Entire Contents." One arrowed sign by the "Good Riddance Girls" caught my eye. It promised a great sale, it started at 9:00 A.M. with "NO EARLY BIRDS!" and it was a half-mile away. I followed the trail of arrows and found myself among dozens of cars parked willy-nilly on the residential street. A line of folks, shoppers-in-waiting, stood along the sidewalk of a neatly landscaped mid-century ranch house, reading newspapers and playing eye gymnastics with their competition.

"You're Seventeen," Sixteen informed me as I took my place in line behind her and her friend, Fifteen. Sixteen and Fifteen were lively women in their mid-fifties, who obviously lived by the belief that the higher the hair the closer to God. I loved them instantly.

"The Good Riddance Girls have the best sales," Sixteen crowed, sipping from a large Dunkin' Donuts travel mug.

DUNKIN' DONUTS
Dunkin' Donuts serves almost 1 billion cups of coffee a year. That's 2.7 million cups of coffee a day, enough coffee cups in a year to circle the earth more than twice.

"Good prices," Fifteen agreed. "And they only take a sale if it has good stuff. They don't waste their time." As we waited, Fifteen and Sixteen graciously got me up to speed on the estate and tag sale branch of saling. Since they were ahead of me in line, they knew I wasn't going to get what they wanted.

I learned that tag sale organizers like the Good Riddance Girls work on commission, getting 25 percent of sales for taking the angst out of selling the contents of an estate ("often after someone dies, gets divorced, or heads to a nursing home"). For shoppers, the experience is dreamy one-stop shopping: from basement to attic, bedroom to bathroom. Everything is for sale—from Tupperware lids to bedroom sets.

Organizers typically put a sign-up sheet outside about an hour before the sale is to begin, and, for crowd control and to prevent shoplifting or price tag switching, shoppers are called inside in order, ten or so at a time. For good sales, the line actually forms before dawn, and the first to arrive traditionally keeps the pre-list list. Fifteen told me that One had arrived at two in the morning, and Two had arrived shortly thereafter. "They're dealers," Sixteen whispered. "I've seen them buy Tiffany lamps for twenty dollars."

"There'll be nothing left by the time we get in," I fretted.

"Don't worry," Fifteen assured me. "You'll get good stuff. They're looking for specific things, like Chippendale chairs."

"And Lalique," Sixteen said. "That one likes Lalique."

As the clock ticked toward nine, the anticipation was palpable. Even in the cool spring morning air, I was sweating.

The first ten were let in promptly at nine. The rest of us stood outside anguished over what they were nabbing. One by one, as the early treasure hunters came out triumphantly showcasing their cache, others were let in. Number Two walked past us proudly carrying a stained glass lamp as if it

ARE YOU INTO LALIQUE?

René Lalique is recognized as one of the world's greatest glassmakers and jewelry designers of the art nouveau and art deco periods, renowned for his stunning creations of perfume bottles, vases, jewelry, chandeliers, clocks, and, in the latter part of his life, automobile hood ornaments. Many of his jewelry pieces and vases showcase plants, flowers, and flowing lines. He was responsible for the walls of lighted glass and the elegant glass columns that filled the dining room and grand salon of the SS *Normandie*. The firm he founded is still active and his early work is highly sought after.

This piece, *Rooster*, is by René Lalique.

10 Steps to a Good Deal

1. Build a relationship with the seller. A little humor while shopping goes a long way.

2. Make a reasonable offer based on what you know you can pay. (Offering $1 on an item priced $20 is insulting and will probably create ill will.)

3. After getting a feel for the pricing structure, gather your items before asking the seller for a group price.

4. Keep your poker face on.

5. Decide what you can live without before you negotiate.

6. Ask for the seller's best price or ask "Would you take x?" rather than insulting the seller's price or saying, "I can get it elsewhere for less."

7. Negotiate a compromise; for example, if you have $100 in your pocket and the "best price" is $125, ask if that would work.

8. If the seller insists on $125, show your money and ask what your $100 could buy.

9. Hope the dealer says, "You can have it all."

10. Either pay the agreed on price, dump the less desired items, or be prepared to walk away.

were the Olympic torch. Fifteen and Sixteen disappeared into the house without so much as a good-bye.

By the time my number was called, I had forgotten my limitations—small apartment and smaller rental car—and went wild. I wanted everything, especially anything already wearing a red SOLD sign. Everybody wants what everybody wants. I raced around the house, affixing SOLD signs to numerous things. A woman talked me out of a mink coat with a glaringly rational argument: "I really want it, and I AM a woman." As a male vegetarian, I bought her argument, and she bought a perfect-condition, full-length mink for $200!

At the end of the spree, I had only spent $145 and gotten a sixties-era kitchen table and matching orange swivel chairs, a dresser (filled with vintage men's clothes), a couple of plants, and a few boxes of assorted vintage relics. I had also placed a lowball bid on a velvet sofa into the "bid box." Two trips and a van rental later I got everything home, including the sofa.

ROAD TRIPS
THE WORLD'S LARGEST GARAGE SALE

Being "the biggest" is just about as good as it gets in America. Basically, when it comes to sales, size can matter. If a single-family garage sale is good, a thousand-family garage sale is mind-blowingly great. The big sales are to salers like theme parks to teenagers and candy stores to kids—a destination where we know we'll get a great rush.

The *Guinness Book of World Records* has deemed the annual Warrensburg Garage Sale in upstate New York the World's Largest Garage Sale. Started in 1979, it's the granddaddy of community-wide garage sales and happens the weekend before Columbus Day every fall. During the two days, over one thousand vendors set up shop in the tiny Adirondack town of Warrensburg, and the population swells from around five thousand to one hundred thousand.

The Warrensburg sale is either a garage sale lover's dream or nightmare because there is so much to see you can never get to it all, even in two days. Since the entire surrounding area has hitched on to the sale—from Lake George to the south to miles north into the Adirondacks—the event has become a giant ten-mile labyrinth of crisscrossing paths and passages into sales in yards, beneath tents, on side streets, and in churches (where early in the morning I bought a delicious McMethodist muffin sandwich).

Recently I went with my friend John Krenek, an interior designer and owner of

Spruce, a mid-century modern furniture store in New York. Most people go to garage sales to buy items for their personal use, but more and more people are going to find objects to re-sell in shops, on eBay, or, like John, for clients.

"I go at it with a very open mind," he told me as we drove north on the New York State Thruway. "I never know what I'm looking for. It's truly about the mix, and how it's put together. In designing, I love throwing in something unexpected, and I often find that piece, something unique and special, at a yard sale. When you see it, you know what it is. It's that thing that puts the perfect finishing touch on a room, brings it all together."

Legend has it . . . the first yard sale was held by Clara Ford, who was so frustrated with husband Henry's collection of tools and junk that she tossed it into the yard and let people buy it.

As we approached the exit, John announced, "We've got to plan our attack. I remember this one sale in a ritzy section of the Hamptons that didn't start until noon. So I stared at all this fabulous stuff from the road and planned for two hours exactly how I'd race through. It was that good. I knew when they opened the gates it would be a mad frenzy. My heart was racing so fast I thought I was going to die. I grabbed treasures left and right, and

that night I drove back to the city with a forties' French desk on top of the car like a bagged deer, feeling like I had hit the jackpot, won Lotto."

We headed into town the night before the sale, so we could scout the area and strategize. We noted where we would park—a central spot so that we could dump our finds and run for more—and we decided where we'd begin and when. "How does five-thirty A.M. sound?" John suggested.

"Getting here, or waking up?" I asked.

"Getting here, of course."

"I'm all about it." Even though I had never gone saling with John, we were kindred spirits.

By 6:00 A.M. on Saturday morning there were several hundred of the tried and true parked and combing the streets for early deals. Before seven, we had already made a trip back to the car to dump our first load.

There were people with Walkie-Talkies, performing a "breaker breaker 1-9" reconnaissance mission on prices. There was one lady inspecting things with a magnifying glass like she was a forensic scientist at a crime scene. There were numerous people reading the bottoms of dishware into cell phones as if they held the secret combination to a treasure chest. "May I ask who you were calling?" I said to one man after he finished reading the bottom of a vase to someone on the phone.

"My wife," he explained. "She's typing things into eBay and telling me how much they're going for."

I'm not that kind of buyer. In fact, in most circumstances, I don't care what other people would pay for something. It's what I would pay for it. "I'm obviously an emotional buyer," I said to John as we moved through a crowd of people loaded down like pack mules. "How much would I pay for the thrill of sitting on it? Wearing it? Looking at it every day? Using it? Giving it to someone?"

John agreed, "Decorating and being drawn to a particular style or thing operates on the same principle as buying art—some people like abstract, some people like realism—just buy the flavor you like. And pay what it's worth to you."

We ran into several sellers who exalted what their items would sell for on eBay, to which I always responded, "Then why aren't you selling it on eBay? You'll have 150 million buyers instead of just me." One man went as far as explaining the ins and outs of trickle-down and supply-side economics before telling me that his metal robot, which "may or may not be a repro," was well priced at $200. "They aren't making them anymore," he said, forgetting his prior statement, "They're getting good at making 'em look old." I passed. If the robot had been an authentic fifties toy made in Japan, which I'd bet it wasn't, it could sell for upward of $1,000. If it was a reproduction, it was overpriced by $150.

My theory on pricing is that if a seller knows the brand name and collectibility factor of something he's selling but says he isn't sure if it's real or a reproduction, it's definitely repro. And in my experience if sellers "don't know if it works" or "haven't tried it," they do, they have, and it doesn't.

In a booth near Warrensburg Town Hall, I admired the humor of the Andee's Anteeks sign and journeyed up a small hill to see what was inside Andee's big white tent. Andy Seyfried was meticulous in his setup and pricing, and heartfelt in his selling. "My favorite thing to sell," the retired engi-

Beware of Reproductions

If something is in demand as a collectible, someone is going to try to make a fake. Repronews.com is an online database of fakes and reproductions and puts out a monthly report of Fakes, Frauds, and Facts. If you're spending money for a collectible, you want to make sure to be able to recognize a fraud.

neer said, as I admired his collection of toys, "is something someone buys for their child because they remember it from their own childhood and now hope that their own child will keep it forever. A little while ago, this adorable tow-headed boy—must have been about six or seven—fell in love with an old scooter I had. It was his birthday, and I heard him tell his mother he wanted it as his present. I told her she could have a discount.

"She bought it, and that little fella's eyes got so big. When I unhooked it from the post I had it on, I asked him if he knew how to ride a scooter, and he nodded his head. I said, 'Well then, you should ride it out of here, shouldn't you?' That kid's smile made my whole day. Maybe my whole year. He'll always remember it."

As I made my way over to his dollar table, Andy continued, "Last week, another neat thing happened. This nice girl bought a nice sewing-room stand, mahogany with two shelves. When she

Andy Seyfried is the best kind of seller—he's very knowledgeable and he really cares about his buyers. "I give a money-back guarantee. If you buy something for someone and they don't like it, you can bring it back and, as long as it's not damaged, I'll refund your money. Only one person has ever brought anything back and that was because it didn't fit in the house."

backed her car up, it wouldn't fit. She was devastated. I found out she lives upstate a few miles from where my father-in-law has a camp, so I told her I'd bring it to her. She was so happy. She paid for it, no receipt or anything, just a trust thing. I love that."

Admiring his many incredible finds, I wondered aloud how sellers could let go of their treasures. "It's why I could never be a seller," I said.

"I had a little Civil War–era flask that I sort of miss," Andy said. "But I don't know if there's anything I wouldn't get rid of."

"Nothing?" I asked.

"I better say my wife," he laughed. "Oh, and anything that I acquired from my family. I would never sell anything that I got from my mother or father."

Later, at the sale next to Andee's, I wondered to myself why some people can't let things go. "That's my dad's old *Playboy* collection," the seller blurted out as I thumbed through a box of magazines marked "$12." "I think there's fifty-three of them, but fyi, there's one *Playgirl* in there . . . and my mom says it's not hers."

On Sunday, a woman in line for nachos told me that the unofficial motto of the World's Largest Garage Sale was "seek and ye shall find." With the lack of room in both my stomach and my car's trunk, I'd buy that (or eat it if it was fried and covered in cheese and ketchup). I bought a lot, except a stunning farmhouse sink that someone else had gotten to first.

John found some treasures, including a late-nineteenth-century bearskin sleigh blanket that would the following week be shot for a magazine feature on one of his design projects. We actually found two: one for John, the other for one of his clients. John also found a 1940 edition of the *Boy Scouts of America Handbook for Boys*. "I love it," he said, as we walked back toward the car carrying our treasures. "It's signed by 'Herbert,' the original little Scout who used it, and it'll be the perfect thing on the bedroom nightstand in my guest cabin. It's an unexpected surprise for a guest to settle into bed and discover."

Garage Sale Munchies

At the World's Largest Garage Sale, and all other "event" garage sales, there is no shortage of food. It's an integral part of the fairlike atmosphere. Food vendors fry up chicken wings next to food vendors slicing bloomin' onions behind food vendors grilling racks of ribs, with food vendors powdering fried funnel cakes around the corner for dessert. The smell that wafts through the streets is fried, barbequed delight with sugar sprinkles on top. If you ever thought about buying fat, look no further. If you've thought about dieting, forget it. And if you really want to make the dough, become a food vendor. They rake in the cash and have an all-you-can-eat buffet.

The night before the World's Largest Garage Sale, a waitress at The Grist Mill, the fanciest restaurant in town, told me I had to try the soup in a bread bowl. "They set up in the funeral home parking lot," she said. "And I have to go by there a couple of times. Y-U-M." The line for "soup in a bread bowl" was always longer than three hearses, so we settled for bloomin' onions, handcut French fries with cheese, nachos (also with cheese), ice cream, elephant ears, funnel cakes (yes, I know they are basically the same thing, but I had to taste both to prove it), and several other delicious artery cloggers.

Based on my own indulgences and crowd size, a conservative estimate for the two-day event is that 1,359,145,840 calories were consumed.

Foods Found at the World's Largest Garage Sale

banana splits	chicken on a stick	corn on the cob	hamburgers	pizza
BBQ chicken	chicken on pita	cotton candy	hot dogs	Polish sausage
BBQ ribs	chicken sandwich	deep-fried Oreos	ice cream cones	popcorn
biscotti	chicken tenders	elephant ears	ice cream floats	pretzels
bloomin' onions	chicken wings	egg rolls	McMethodist	roasted peanuts
burgers	chili	French fries	muffin	snow cones
candy apples	chili dogs	fried dough	nachos	soup bowl
caramel corn	cinnamon rolls	frozen bananas	pastries	sweet potato fries
cheese on a stick	corn dogs	funnel cakes	pecans	turkey legs

ARE YOU INTO HOT WHEELS?

The most popular toy to collect is the Hot Wheels car. It is the only toy that attracts two thousand people to semi-annual collectors' conventions. And many collectors actually attend the conventions for the seven full days. The fortieth model year for Hot Wheels is 2007.

Mattel's early Hot Wheels toy cars (1968–1977) are known as the Redlines because their tires have a red line around the rim. A 1968 Custom Mustang Hot Wheel with a special hood where the hood scoops are open and with an open hood can sell for lots of money, as it was mostly available in the 1968 Strip Action Set. It has only been sold in a blister package as a single car a handful of times. The last one sold for $15,000. A loose one will sell for $200 even in poor condition, but fakes exist because the hoods can be bought and painted to match an original car.

Police, fire, and construction vehicles, while not as pricey, are always in demand. And according to David Williamson at Toycarcollector.com, don't be fooled by the date on the bottom. It was when the mold was created, not when it was made.

With that, and my last purchase of six state plates for $5, we decided to call our expedition done. As we left town, we made several "just one more" stops. But our truly last stop was perhaps the most special, not because of what we bought but because of who we bought from.

Eleven-year-old Lance Bedell was standing on the side of Schroon River Road wearing an orange traffic cone as a hat and waving his arms. It was the kind of attention-getting display that would make people either veer off the road, call 911, or do as I did and find a place to park. As I jaunted across the road, the young man moved into position behind his array of brightly colored, previously enjoyed toys.

"That cone sure stops traffic," I told him.

"Yeah," he grinned. "I've got a few tricks to attract customers. I've found people like that sort of thing. Oh, and my green hair. That stopped a few people. One lady said she turned around because of my hair and then paid me five dollars for a big fat gorilla I won in a raffle."

"Why are you selling your stuff?" I asked him.

"I want to get rid of some stuff like my old junk snowboard," he said, his youthful honesty refreshing. "Well, it really isn't junk, but the only way I could stop myself was by planting my face right in the snow. It hasn't sold, so I'm still stuck with it."

"How much is it?" I asked.

"Five dollars," he said. "Most of my things are five dollars because I'm sort of laid back about my pricing. I get hyped up when I'm selling something, and I'm not sure how much something is supposed to be."

"How much is the little wheelbarrow?" I asked, envisioning it on my front porch with a potted geranium.

"Five dollars?" he asked back, obviously fearing a negotiation. "I started to paint it, but decided to sell it instead. Do you like it?"

Best $5 I ever spent.

Lance Bedell, eleven, is the youngest seller at the World's Largest Garage Sale. According to Lance's mother, Michelle, he's been doing the sale since he was seven: "Lance sold for the Cub Scouts and caught the fever. He's been doing the sale ever since. He thinks he's going to get rich. Last year he caused a bit of a family war when he sold a huge box full of Matchbox cars to a teacher for five bucks. Unfortunately, many of the ones he sold belonged to his brother. There were easily a hundred or so in there and, let's just say, I don't think we've quite gotten over that."

The World's Oldest
Garage Saler

I met ninety-year-old Wini Williams at her garage sale. "Whoever the hell heard of a ninety-year-old woman doing this?" she asked me as she lifted a box from her trunk. "It keeps me alive. Can you hold my canes? I'm setting up a dollar table. Oh, and as you see, I've got to make more shelves. But I'm settling in."

Wini's been garage saling since she was thirty, and knows how to spot a burning good find. "A million years ago when I was young," she remembers with a wink, "Emmaline Miller's Chicken Coop was the first sale I ever remember going to, and then, in the late thirties, I went to Harry Newell's garage sale pretty regularly." She slowly worked to unpack her dollar box. "But my first big sale myself was of a pie chest. I used to go to the dump down the road pretty regularly. At least once a day. My husband came home one day, and said, 'There's a pie chest at the dump that's on fire. You might like it.'

"I went running down there, and stomped the flames out with my boots until they melted. I still have those boots and wear them sometimes; they're just a little flattened out. Well, who would have thrown that in the burn pile? I drug that thing back home, opened it up, and it had a lot of nice stuff in the there, including those Mohonk postcards over there. There were about sixteen hundred of them. I think they got thrown out because the picture was printed backward. I sell them for a dollar and that stack of twenty or so is all I've got left. That's a pretty good return on your money.

"I have to get rid of some of this stuff," she said, looking around the little garage she'd recently built with her own hands so she could set up shop. "That chest is forty dollars; it used to be one hundred twenty. If you're looking for a good deal, that's a good deal.

"But that's not the story . . . I get distracted sometimes. Anyway, that pie chest I pulled from the fire was Pennsylvania Dutch, and I sold it for a quick six hundred dollars. I put some of the proceeds to help restore Walt Whitman's house in Huntington. Long Island, Exit 110. I got my lilacs from his property." I later learned that in 1949 Wini helped start the campaign to save Walt Whitman's birthplace and had sales to raise money for its rescue.

Newsday, Long Island's daily newspaper, began a campaign requesting a dollar donation, and schoolchildren collected pennies, nickels, and dimes. All in all, $33,000 were raised and the birthplace of America's greatest poet is today a historic site and attracts thousands each year from around the world.

A gentleman came into Wini's garage and clanked through her pile of Griswold frying pans, like one my grandmother gave me for all the cornbread I don't make. "How much is this?" he asked, holding up a particularly well-seasoned pan.

FRYING PANS
Griswold, founded in 1865, is the original cast iron frying pan company. Its pans (well seasoned, of course) command high prices on eBay.

"What do you want to offer me?" Wini countered.

"Five."

"You think I'm stupid," she cracked. "I'll take ten." And the deal was done.

"I'm a natural salesman," she told me after he left. "I used to sell china in the china department at A&S in Hempstead. I sold more Lennox than anyone. I'd take Lennox teacups and stand on them to show they wouldn't break. I was a Jean Harlow type, with bleached blonde hair, real brazen. You get the picture, a good-looking blonde standing on teacups. It was a real show and would always gather a crowd. I was working on commissions, and it was like I had fallen into a barrel of money."

Wini was a millionaire by the time she was thirty.

"I work every night until 2 A.M. on this stuff. Why would I sleep? There's too much for me to do than die. I'm doing it forever."

THE WORLD'S LONGEST YARD SALE

The predawn hours awaiting the start of the World's Longest Yard Sale is a toss and a turn, much like the early morning hours of every childhood Christmas. As a child I'd wrestle with the sheets, waiting for the time I could rouse the rest of the house to go discover what toys Santa had left for us good kids. As an adult awaiting the World's Longest Yard Sale, the feeling is the same. Just how early does an "early bird" have to be to get the tastiest worm at the World's Longest Sale? If I'm not the first in line, will the others—oh, there will be others—grab exactly what I want? The perfect thingamajig, the coolest thingamabob, and the exact doodad I need for my doodad collection.

The U.S. 127 Sale at 450 miles is no longer officially the country's longest sale—the Great U.S. 50 Yard Sale goes coast to coast and is 3,073 miles, though there are sometimes hundreds of miles between sales. But the U.S. 127 Sale is unquestionably the longest sale with the most jam-packed population of sellers. In fact, it is an oddity to drive a mile of the 450 miles without a sale.

The sale began in 1987 in Jamestown, Tennessee, by Fentress County Executive Mike Walker, who came up with the idea as a way to entice travelers off the interstates and onto the back roads. It worked. Each year, the first Thursday to Sunday in August, thousands of sellers set up shop and cater to hundreds of thousands of shoppers. The sales are so abundant and tempting, it is sometimes hard to drive a mile in an hour, much less go the entire five-state route in four days.

The thought of mile after mile, state after state of sale has become for many a goal as ambitious as climbing Mount Everest or as monumental as jumping out of a plane. For two decades, people have come from around the world to drive the route and pluck treasures from countless roadside sales.

It's my turn, I thought, as I wrestled within the crunchy sheets of the Highway Inn in Gadsden, Alabama. The Highway Inn is not its real name, but it was right on a highway, and it was in Gadsden, Alabama—the

Do's and Don'ts for Sellers

Do

- Price your goods fairly.

- Realize that you're getting rid of things you don't want and price accordingly.

- Use price tags that won't damage items or boxes.

- Have a sense of humor. "Holler if you don't like a price" works nicely.

- Have tape measure and electric outlet available. People like to measure and to check working condition.

- Mark items that aren't for sale.

- Clean your items.

- Set up your items like you're a store. People need to see items to buy them.

- Wash and hang clothes if you want to sell them.

- Inform buyers if you know something doesn't work.

- Tell your neighbors. They might even join in.

- Provide bags.

- Give your leftovers to charity. See if the charity will pick up donated items.

Don't

- Act as if you're operating a museum. People touch things at garage sales.

- Be greedy.

- Be crabby.

- Sell broken things.

- Sell things from the 99¢ store for a dollar.

- Sell something you don't own.

- Ask "new" prices for used things.

- Think because you don't want it that no one else does.

- Sell your family heirlooms unless you're willing to let go of them forever.

- Quote eBay or book values. Nobody cares.

southernmost starting point of the 450-mile yard sale that each August, as sure as the trade winds, winds its way up from Alabama, into northernmost Georgia, and then onto Route 127 through Tennessee, Kentucky, and into Cincinnati, Ohio.

I was joined for the journey by my friend Beverly Saponaro, a vintage kitchenware expert, and my decorating spiritual advisor of sorts. Bev transformed her garage into my favorite vintage store in the Catskills, Cathouse Antiques, and with her good taste and great eye, I knew she'd be the perfect Bonnie to my Clyde for the trip. We promised each other we'd get as far as we could until we either ran out of money or the truck got full. Whichever came first. And both were going to last us a while.

Each of us had brought a thousand bucks to burn through. Bev had hers neatly assorted in a fanny pack, and I had $1,000 in ones packed in a bank bag marked "$1000." Yes, one thousand ones in a bag from the Federal Mint. Not only did I feel rich, but I also had faith that those ones were going to help me win friends and influence people by late Saturday or early Sunday when the sellers would have run out of small change. The banks would be closed, and they'd have nowhere to turn except me. It was still the wee hours of Thursday morning but the strategizing had already begun.

Room 217 stunk like an ashtray dipped in vanilla and sprinkled with baby powder. When we arrived, I opened the drapes to find that Room 217 came with a scenic view of the parking lot. Lots of large vehicles were backed up to the building and I made note of their MOs. ANNTEEK from Iowa, SHOPR from North Carolina, and a dented minivan plastered with Garage Sale Junkie bumper stickers, but none of them were as big as ours.

We had flown to Atlanta from New York earlier that afternoon and taken a cab to a Penske dealer across from the Kmart distribution center. "I don't see anything small," Bev noted as our cabbie peeled away. "They all look like they could move a house."

"Don't worry," I reassured her. "I have a confirmed reservation for a little van thing."

"No, sir," Bradley told me, as we stood at the counter, our luggage at our feet. "*Confirmed* means you are confirmed for *a truck*, not necessarily confirmed for the *size* of the truck." Bev stood quietly in the corner, clutching her fanny pack and biting her lower lip. She saw the writing on the wall. We were going to break off every branch on every curvy country road all the way back to New York.

"It's only four feet longer than the one you reserved," Bradley said, stumbling momentarily on the word *reserved*. His associate, David, threw in: "These are the ones the college students drive back to college." I heard don't-be-a-baby undertones.

"While you two decide what kind of deal you're going to give us, my friend Bev and I are going to look at the thing." My negotiating had already begun. I am a garage saler after all, and if I can't find a good deal, I'm mov-

ing on. "What do you think?" I asked Bev as we sat inside the cab. "Can we drive this thing?"

"What else can we do?" she asked, looking around at the industrial wasteland outside the windshield. "I mean, where else are we going to go?"

It was a white-knuckled drive at first. The Beast had more mirrors than a beauty pageant, but after a few near misses with objects that were *much* closer than they appeared and a couple of squashed pylons in a construction zone, I got over it. I suppose, after all was said and done, we had scored the deal of the century, with two dozen moving blankets and a sturdy-looking lock thrown in for free! The deal was unbelievably good.

I patted myself on the back and rolled out of bed. "Let's go, Bev! We have the World's Longest Yard Sale to get to, in the world's biggest truck."

WAFFLE HOUSE
If you could stack all of the sausage patties Waffle House serves in one day, it would reach the top of the Empire State Building in New York City.

Between drags of her chain-lit menthol, Jan, seated familiarly atop the third stool at the Waffle House in Gadsden, Alabama, gave us directions on how to get to the starting mile of the World's Longest Yard Sale and added: "I'm not sure I see the whole point in yard saling. I mean why pay ten dollars for a crappy old lawn chair when you can buy a brand new one at Wal-Mart for $9.98."

"I love people like Jan," I told Bev as I turned the behemoth right toward Mecca. "She makes it so much easier for the rest of us."

It was not yet eight in the morning, but by the time we neared the starting point—a park with a couple pavilions and two fields of row after row of merchandise—there were enough other disciples to slow traffic to a crawl. We attracted attention. No one's truck was as big. And ours was banana yellow. At the starting point, I squeezed the truck into three parking spaces, leaving enough room to make an escape without the need for reverse.

DAY ONE
MILE ZERO, FIELD ONE

Bev and I leapt out of the truck and sprinted toward the pavilions. There were people darting around tarps and in and out of the pavilions like ants at a picnic. The two pavilions were, of course, the high-end real estate. Location, location, location. Whether rain or sun, the metal-roofed pavilions would provide protection for shoppers, sellers, and their merchandise. We figured since these sellers had paid extra for the privilege, they had confi-

dence both that their stuff was good and that they had a lot of it. Bev and I entered the first pavilion and headed in opposite directions. Bev left me for a table full of Bakelite. I was lured by bait.

Jim Partain and his wife had their sale smartly showcased in a two-tiered display on the top and benches of a row of picnic tables. His wife's collection of costume jewelry took the north end of the table, but it was Jim's fishing tackle on the south end that immediately caught my attention. "There's some oldie-goldies there," he said reeling me in. "They were my grandfather's, Earley Partain, named after a Civil War general." He could see the early-morning hungriness in my eyes. "You like to fish?" My extensive knowledge of lures and fishing involves one ill-fated trip with my dad in

ARE YOU INTO BAKELITE?

Belgium-born chemist Leo Baekeland used his $1,000,000 profit from the sale of Velox to Eastman Kodak to set up a lab in Yonkers. While working on a durable coating for the lanes of bowling alleys, he created what is considered to be the first plastic by mixing carbolic acid with

formaldehyde. After a decade of industrial applications, Bakelite entered the consumer market in the form of decorative handles, drinking glasses, musical instruments, and jewelry.

Bakelite became fashionable during the Depression because of its low cost and bright colors. Today, objects made from Bakelite are considered highly collectible. Intricately carved Bakelite jewelry with polka dots and in fancy shapes can run into the thousands of dollars.

Buyer beware! Bakelite fakes are out there. Here's how to tell the real from the fake:

1. The weight of Bakelite is heavier than plastic. Compare the weight of something plastic of similar size.
2. Scratches and patina come with age and with use. Old pieces of Bakelite will show some minor scratching and wear, while plastic will look new.
3. Tap two pieces of Bakelite together. They make a solid clunking sound, rather than the clinking sound of plastic.
4. Either pour scalding water over the item or vigorously rub to build heat. Smell it while it's still hot. Stink like burning hair? It's Bakelite.

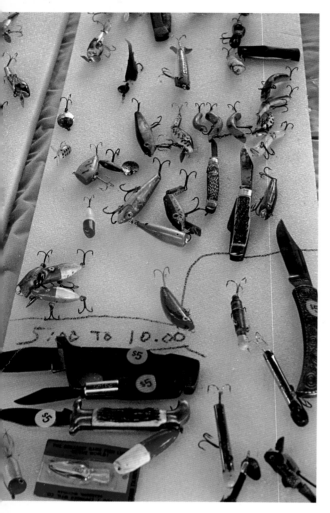

which I refused to pierce a worm with the hook, even though he assured me the worm wouldn't feel it. By the way it squirmed, I had the feeling he was dead wrong.

"I'm attracted to the lures, I suppose, from a fish's perspective," I told Jim. "I think they're beautiful." I examined the teeny works of art, understanding quickly how unsuspecting prey might be tempted to try a taste. They are dangerously enticing, like a charringly hot light bulb to a fluttering moth in the dark of night. Jim told me his father died in 1979 and left him his grandfather's lure collection. This year, while cleaning out his shed, Jim decided "they finally had to go."

"Now, don't get hooked," Jim warned. "They'll get ya." I wasn't sure if he meant literally or figuratively, but they had already "gotten" me. I wanted every one of them. "The one you're holding is a broken-back mirror lure. It's good for bass. They have that shine to them." By the time Jim was done with me, I had bought his favorites, his oldest, and a few that had caught my eye for $31. He wrapped them inside a Piggly Wiggly plastic grocery store bag and wished me good luck fishing. Three towns later I would discover a fishing-lure expert who was selling one like mine for $350.

TAKE A LOOK AT SALES IN . . . *Maine* shortly before Labor Day Weekend when all the rich folk with summer homes decide to travel light and say good-bye to their luxury goods. The recycling center, a.k.a. "the dump," is often home to a bounty of lawn furniture, bicycles, and other big pieces that won't fit in the car.

The Lure Expert

Lure-collector Robbie Pavey created Mrlurebox.com, which provides a wealth of information about antique lures. His life-long love of lures started with a special tackle box. "When I was a kid, my grandfather had a great big double-sided Kennedy metal tackle box with a dome top, which he kept in his fishing closet. The fishing closet was in the basement of his house, under the stairwell, and it was very special for the grandchildren to get to peek in there.

"Every now and then, he'd dig some things out of there and take me fishing. One day in my mid-teens he gave me that tackle box. I fished with (and lost) a lot of those lures and still have a couple of them. They are probably worth four or five dollars total, but they have priceless meaning to me.

"By the time I was in twelfth grade, I was picking through stuff at yard sales looking for lures. They have a beautiful history, and best of all you could find them. You still can. A lot of collectibles—coins, stamps, Barbies—are manufactured, so you have to wait until the maker puts them on the market. Fishing lures are readily available at most garage sales.

"The most important lure company in American history was started in the late eighteen hundreds by James Heddon, who was a leading apiarist (beekeeper), politician, and newspaper publisher. The oft-told legend holds that Heddon was waiting for a fishing partner one afternoon at the Old Mill Pond near the town of Dowagiac. He tossed a whittled 'plug' of wood into the still water and was startled when a bass struck it violently. Thus, the idea for a top-water bait was born."

Antique lures have always been highly valued, Robbie explained. "Fishing lures are utilitarian. They weren't made to be works of art, they just are. In the early days of fishing lures, what we call the 'Golden Age,' 1900 to 1918, lures cost seventy-five cents to a dollar apiece. That was a big chunk of change. So, the gentlemen of yesteryear took great care of their lures, cleaning them after each use. Today's fishermen consider the plastic lures almost disposable.

"The workmanship that went into these things is incredible. What brings up memories of good times more than a display of antique fishing lures? It goes without saying that I've personally harvested some wonderful treasures at yard sales over the years. There are still lots of good baits that turn up in unexpected places on Saturday mornings—especially if you take the time to ask."

Lures

Lures definitely live up to their name. Their colors, shapes, and design are enticing, and attract creatures with gills and collectors without, including a lot of non-fishermen.

Wee Dee, Creek Chub Bait Co.
Garrett, Indiana

One of the all-time classic lures. The buglike plug with single hooks and wire antennas was short-lived, dating to 1936, and is one of the most sought-after lures of all time.

Hinckley "Yellow Bird" Fish Phantom
Newark, New Jersey

Livingston Hinckley patented the Fish Phantom in 1897. The aluminum, revolving-head baits shimmer as they flutter through the water.

Worden Combination Minnow
Worden Bait Co., South Bend, Indiana

Sometime around 1900, F. G. Worden began making and selling his wooden Minnows, which had all the characteristics of a basic wooden minnow with the added feature of a tied tail hackle.

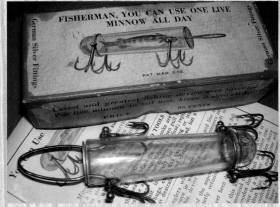

Detroit Glass Minnow Tube
Detroit, Michigan

These well-made, heavy glass lures were marketed around 1914 with the idea that a single minnow could live inside the tube all day and catch fish after fish.

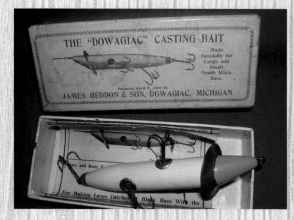

The Dowagiac Casting Bait,
James Heddon & Son
Dowagiac, Michigan

This first Heddon lure is the earliest, and most important, of all Heddon lures. Note the gold-washed cups, chalky white paint, and early white picture box.

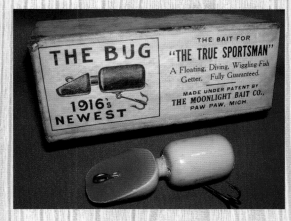

The Bug,
Moonlight Bait Company
Paw Paw, Michigan

These wondrous lures were crafted by Horace Ball and Charles Varney of the Moonlight Bait Company in the basement of the courthouse where Horace worked as a janitor.

The Vann Clay Retrievable Minnow,
Clay's Bait Co.
Thomasville, Georgia

These hollow lures made in the late twenties have an internal spring that enables the head to pull away from the body when snagged, then snap back, hopefully unsnagging the lure.

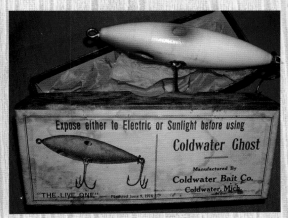

Coldwater Ghost, Coldwater Bait Co.
Coldwater, Michigan

Sometime around 1913, Sam Larrabee of Coldwater, Michigan, received a patent on one of the first wooden plugs whose action was dependent upon water forced through a hole in the chin that then exited on the sides or belly.

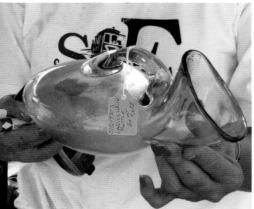

After quickly dropping off our finds at the truck, Bev and I rushed out into the field where glassware, sparkling in the sun, grabbed my attention. I made my way to a woman standing between two tables of an extensive collection of glassware—from tableware to a few unusual pieces. She lifted a vaselike jug off the table and asked me if I knew what it was. "Yes," I said, having bought a similar one for a friend as a urological joke. "It's a glass bedpan."

"Of course," she smiled, "But do you know whose it is?" I thought for a minute she was going to name some aging hoofer like Carol Channing.

"Look at the mouth," she said, pointing to the unique opening. "How do you use it?"

My eyes got as wide as her Depression glass plates. "Oh. Gotcha. It's for a woman, right?"

"Yep," she said proudly, showing me the tag, which clearly proclaimed: 1930s Ladies Urine Bottle, $50.

"You'll never see another one."

I hope not. There are some things you can never unsee.

Across the field, I noticed a woman wearing a shirt covered in a comic book pattern who was yelling, "Want to see my naked chicken?" The naked chicken was made entirely out of grocery store bags, of the "Paper or plastic?" variety. "Kroger bags," she volunteered proudly. "See? See right there." She pointed to a faint blue logo about the size of a dime on the chicken's back.

She sold recycled art, which was hard to miss, and her name was She-She, which was hard to forget.

"It's folk art," she said, her eyes twinkling. "What do you think I make it out of?"

"Let's see," I said, examining her colorful works more closely. "Looks like barn wood. And that's a shingle . . ."

"What I use," she drawled, circling her flat palm over several paintings.

"Paint?" I analyzed. "And maybe some grits."

"Yep," She-She nodded. "Blue grits and stone-ground grits. But that's not what I'm talking about." I was stumped and my face showed it. I loved her whimsy and the boldness of her colors, but for the life of me, I couldn't figure out what the heck she was getting at. "It's house paint and mud," she finally blurted, taking a quick nibble on her lower lip, "from my catfish pond!"

I admired She-She's art and took some photos of *Pink-Chicken-Rooster*©. Legend has it that *Pink-Chicken-Rooster*© wanted to be a flamingo so badly that he became one. Moral of the story? "Never give up on your dreams." And eat a lot of flamingo food.

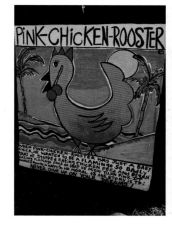

Folk artist She-She, from Birmingham, Alabama, uses recycled materials and words of wisdom—"You must give to others . . . so that opportunity might come your way"—in her uplifting art for the soul. "It's cedar from my back porch," she told me. "It collapsed, so I decided to use the wood."

77

Garage Sale Artists

Jamie Midgley, photographer, Raintree Gallery, High Falls, New York

His work is a collaborative effort thanks to helpful friends. "Elizabeth and Aidan Quinn were always finding things at garage sales and giving them to me. So, I decided to start incorporating my photography into these found objects. Aidan bought an old radiator from a 1945 Ford truck, and I made that into a sculptural piece that lights up. He was just coming off his TV show *The Book of Daniel*, so we put Jesus on the dashboard. It's a fabulous piece that he has in his office at home.

"Lizzy gave me a light rim as a birthday gift and said, 'I'm sure you'll find something to do with this!' It took a while to come up with an idea that would work for the light rim, then it made perfect sense to build a photograph around it, and create a theme using the piece as a light and bring a dead car alive.

"Everything I do is a collaboration, and I love that. Steve Heller, who has a store near Woodstock called Fabulous Furniture, creates incredible things out of wood and scrap metal. He framed a picture I had taken in New York on a rainy night in corrugated steel. That worked out, so we took these pictures I had taken in Florida on a movie set of a row of rusted out cars and put them into an actual car door we found at a junk sale. It works.

"Now that I've opened the gallery, people are setting me up with all sorts of odd bits and pieces they are finding at sales or on the side of the road. I've had pretty good luck finding a home for these oddities; discovering an extension of what they are. Working my way through the elaborate mystery of what they become is the fun part."

Gordon Carlisle, muralist and sculptor,
South Berwick, Maine

He makes his living primarily as a mural artist in Maine, but yard sale art is a way for him to cut loose and have a little fun on the side. "I go junk-tiquing to yard sales, thrift shops, and our local transfer station with my eyes peeled for items worth augmenting," explains Gordon. "I buy old postcards and magazines and use them to collage, or sometimes just for inspiration. Old paint-by-number paintings are always attractive.

"Things just happen with yard sale items. I love zooming in on them and going with my gut reaction to what I'm looking at. Then it'll hit me: Here's the twist that I have to impose on this object I've found. I'm often not sure what the connection is, but I stick to it. The object triggers something in me, and that's reason enough to buy it.

"*Burnt Offering* came about when I found the original print at a garage sale; it came with the frame. Never in my life had I seen a frame like that. Somebody made it. It was really dirty and nicked a bit, but I knew I could touch it up. The print itself was a vision of the cave. In the background, where you see sky, there was a church there, the sanctuary of Lourdes, and there was Madonna in the Cave. It hit me to put the Great One in her stead. It was a vision: Elvis in the cave being offered up a cheeseburger."

ON THE ROAD

We were finally back in the truck, driving north and watching a line of cars, SUVs, and campers heading to the southernmost tail of the World's Longest Sale where we'd already been. But what had those passing us discovered ahead of our arrival? What had they tucked away in their trunks that I didn't get to first? I couldn't take it anymore. "I'm pulling over at the next spot where I fit," I told Bev.

We'd gone only a quarter mile.

We headed to the lawn of a brick ranch house that was covered in "sale." The owners' items were sitting on the front walk, because they'd rented out every other inch of their yard—the garage, the driveway, the side yard, the other side yard, and the porch—to other sellers. I think they would have rented out space on the roof if it weren't for the fact they had already sold their ladder. These were people who would have sold their grandma, if she weren't having a sale at her own house down the street.

They did have a crowd, though, and some great finds once I got past the guy with the itchy sweaters. I noticed his sweaters straight away strewn across a rented boxwood hedge. They were a matching set—cardigan and pullover—both emblazoned with a letterman's B on the front. Given that my name is Bruce, I naturally thought they were made for me. Until I tried them on. Besides smelling like a wet, ninety-year-old sheep, the current proprietor quoted their "book value at forty dollars."

"You're kidding me, right?" I asked, trying to wiggle out of the wool. "There's a blue book on these?"

Apparently so. I laid the sweater back on the boxwood to await its "B"rad or "B"illy with a bigger wallet and no sense of smell.

On the other side of the yard, Bonnie Langley pulled me out of my woolly funk by waving a set of lime green and pink, hand-beaded placemats. "Two dollars for the set," she announced. "Somebody should buy these. Val from

Junkin' would grab these things up in a skinny second." I don't know Val, but I do know Val-ue. And she's lovely. These were a steal at $2. They screamed 1974 and obviously took some obsessive-compulsive countless hours to complete. "The perfect gift for my friend who still lives in the seventies," I told Bonnie. "Hold it up. Let me get your picture."

"Me at my worst," she laughed. I snapped her picture and handed her $2.

"You already paid me."

"No, I didn't," I said.

"Yes, you did," she insisted, trying to hand me back the money. I refused. We were at a standoff.

"Tell you what," she said. "Take a dollar back. I'll feel better; you'll feel better."

I was a little wary that I might somehow have actually made money on the deal, but I did feel better. And I got great placemats before Junkin' Val showed up.

Also at Bonnie's table, Natalie Johnson had just scored a great deal. The ten-year-old from Moulton, Alabama, was traveling the World's Longest Yard Sale as a vacation trip with her grandparents. (Grandpa was strictly the driver, he assured me.) Natalie had found a not-so-old Barbie and a handful of Barbie clothes for $1, including Barbie's original black-and-white-striped one-piece bathing suit. Her grand-  mother avowed they were going to make the whole 450-mile trip, and Natalie nodded optimistically. Two days later, when we ran into them in Tennessee, Natalie had acquired enough Barbie memorabilia to start a museum. Two months later, Bev would decide to send Natalie her own Barbie collection, including the Barbie box on which she had scrawled "Property of Beverly Fiore" when she was ten.

It is often in these fleeting exchanges that our most everlasting memories are wrapped, tagged, and relished for a lifetime.

How Barbie Came to Be

 In 1959, after a trip to Europe in which she saw the popularity of the lipsticked and shapely Bild Lili doll, Ruth Handler created the most famous doll of the twentieth century and named her Barbie after her daughter Barbara. The first Barbie sold for $3 and wore a strapless black-and-white-striped bathing suit, more makeup than perhaps appropriate, and stood eleven and a half inches tall.

After her introduction at the American Toy Fair, Barbie languished on store shelves until Ruth, wife of the cofounder of Mattel, got the company to start sponsoring commercials on *The Mickey Mouse Club*. Since then, there have been more than a billion Barbies sold; on average two Barbies are sold every second around the world. Today, a mint-condition, original "Barbie #1" has sold for around $10,000.

Fun Barbie Facts

- Barbie's full name is Barbie Millicent Roberts.

- She is from Willows, Wisconsin.

- If Barbie were a real person, her measurements would be 36-18-38.

- The first Barbie with bendable legs was introduced in 1965.

- Barbie's first career was as a teen fashion model, but she has since had more than eighty careers, including a run for president of the United States.

- Ken, introduced in 1961 and named after Ruth's son, has been Barbie's one and only boyfriend.

- The first African-American and Hispanic Barbies were introduced in 1980.

- Wheelchair-bound Share a Smile Becky was introduced in 1997.

- According to Mattel, Totally Hair Barbie, with hair reaching from her head to her toes, was the best-selling Barbie ever.

- Barbie is currently a $1.5 billion-a-year industry.

DAY TWO

SIGNAL MOUNTAIN, TENNESSEE,
TO CROSSVILLE, TENNESSEE

The drive up Signal Mountain was stunning, with beautiful views and lots of interesting houses along a curvy mountain road. There were numerous sales dotting the twists and turns, but I didn't dare pull our gigantic truck off the road for fear I'd go over the edge. When we finally were able to stop in a flat area with a more expansive shoulder, we were rewarded with great finds including a vintage Coca-Cola® reach-in refrigerator ($100), perfect to fill with bottles of champagne and ice for a garden party; an intricately embroidered state flowers quilt ($60); and an amazing thirties-era barber's pole in working condition. At $320, it was my most expensive buy of the trip, but I'd always wanted one and figured I'd never see another.

It was at this stop I met two people who reminded me what the garage sale experience is all about.

Atlantan Dyan Richardson was combing through boxes of comic books. "Do you know anything about comic books?" she asked me.

"Very little," I said. "Do you?"

"Not a thing," she admitted. "But my husband has been griping for years that his mother threw away all his comic books, so I thought I'd put together a collection of them for his birthday."

Thoughtfulness: often a shared trait among those who garage sale. "I think that is probably the case with many mothers," I laughed. Though comic books were printed in huge quantities, they were cheap and were often thrown away or lost and replaced by new ones. "The ones without barcodes are older," I told her, "and I'm not sure if they have them, but anything with a zip code was made after 1963." A comic book collector in Kentucky later told me that the oldest comic books aren't necessarily the most valuable. In fact, though many comic books were introduced in the forties, comic books printed between the early fifties and the late seventies are often the most sought out because collectors prefer comics from their own childhoods. "The condition is important," he said, "But I'd be happy to take a worn copy of any comic book where the hero was introduced."

By the end of her browsing Dyan had a healthy stack—everything from Batman to Porky Pig, Bugs Bunny, and Archie. "That will make him happy," she said with a smile, "then maybe he'll leave me alone!"

Sandra Cochran from Cleveland, Tennessee, was in a spot next door selling buttons and costume jewelry, and epitomized how a passion can become a career for garage salers. "I suppose my business started because my husband was missing a button off his shirt," she said, "But it's turned into something great. I have tens of thousands of buttons and, at any one time, six to eight thousand pieces of costume jewelry."

Her collection was remarkably well organized and as people came into her booth with button questions, she was able to direct them to what they were

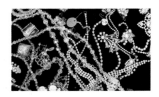

looking for—whether brass, glass, or bone. "I've been taking care of ill relatives," Sandra said, while showing me an art deco brooch that looked like a jewel-encrusted skyscraper. "And I've realized doing this is my therapy. Counting and sorting buttons is very relaxing."

According to Sandra, costume jewelry wasn't made only for people who couldn't afford real jewels. Costume jewelry with its various "jewels" came in a variety of colors and styles, and was made to make the wearer feel special. "None of the pieces are alike," she noted. "The intriguing thing about buttons and costume jewelry is the exclusivity when you wear it. You're not going to meet it coming down the street. I think that's why I like it. It helps us all be original."

FAUX FOLLIES

Though imitation jewels have been worn since the eighteenth century, legend has it that costume jewelry was given its name by Broadway impresario Florenz Ziegfeld, creator of the Ziegfeld Follies. He is said to have ordered imitation jewelry to go with the showy outfits for his Ziegfeld girls and called it their "costume jewelry."

Identifying Buttons

Buttons come in a huge range of materials, from bone to avocado pit, gold, and rubber. Experts give a few hints to identify their origin; for example:

Bone: It has pockmarks that look like little splinters, and a coarse, porous texture.

Horn: It smells like roasting meat when heated. Rapidly rub the button with your finger to build heat.

Tortoiseshell: It smells like dirty water or dead fish when heated, so rapidly rub the button with your finger to build heat.

Pewter and **Steel:** Pewter will not magnetize, steel will, so use a magnet to verify the button material.

Gold and **Silver:** Have a jeweler perform a chemical test if you think your buttons are gold or silver.

Somewhere in the middle of Tennessee we spotted a metal two-seater glider on the other side of the road. I screeched to a halt, traumatizing the woman in front of us who was trying to shove a mannequin in her trunk. Bev jumped out of the truck and scurried across the road. Bev can sell a metal chair faster than kudzu grows. Rusted and old is stylish these days.

Bev casually poked the glider, wiggled it, sat on it—generally gave it a good garage sale tire kicking. I made my approach. Bev gave me the subtle nod, and I walked toward two teenage boys standing by a table filled with odds and ends. "Whose is that?" I asked, pointing toward the glider and making sure not to call it by its scientific name, *glideus maximus*.

"Paw-Paw!" the older one screamed in the general direction of a giant oak.

An old man came from behind the tree and crept toward me like a crab, one shoulder markedly higher than the other. He was gnawing on a barbequed turkey leg, parts of which spilled from his mouth as he grumbled, "Two-fifty!"

"Two dollars and fifty cents?" I asked. "Or two hundred fifty dollars?"

"Dollars," he spewed, then turned and headed back behind the tree. It was clear by his price and his attitude that Paw-Paw was destined to eat turkey legs for the rest of his life on that glider. I quietly moved on along the table. There was a neat oilcan with a flexible spout that I thought might make an interesting vase for flowers. "How much?" I asked the boys, holding up the can.

"Paw-Paw!" the same one yelled. "How much you want for the oilcans?!"

"Twenty!" Paw-Paw hollered from behind the tree.

I moved on down the table where my eyes fixed on a collection of marbles. I remember playing marbles (or pretending to play them) as a kid and they've had a special place in my heart ever since my grandfather gave me the lucky handmade clay shooter his dad had given him.

I looked over the various jars of multicolored orbs, holding them up and watching them sparkle in the sun. I wanted to ask how much, but I couldn't bear the thought of Paw-Paw once again screeching from behind the tree. "You like marbles?" the younger boy asked.

"Yes," I said. "I think they're cool."

The older boy stepped in and, after a quick look around, leaned over the table and said, "You can have a jar for four dollars." The first respectful price of the stop. I pulled out four singles from my right pocket and handed them to him. Without counting, he looked back toward the tree and promptly put the money in his pocket. "There's some good ones in there," he smiled.

ARE YOU INTO MARBLES?

Marbles have been around since the Roman Empire. The earliest marbles were made of marble (hence the name), but also baked clay, flint, and stone. The Venetians introduced glass marbles, and in 1848, the manufacturing process was perfected by father and son German glass blowers Elias and Septimus Greiner.

Marble expert Alan Basinet (Marblealan.com) says that games involving marbles have been around since the birth of civilization—small spheres have been recovered from ancient European and Native American archeological sites. But he suggests the real origin of the marbles we're familiar with today to be late fifteenth century, as European paintings from that period illustrate games involving little orbs. The Dutch seem to have been responsible for the spread of the game, and by the seventeenth century the game had come to America.

Christensen Agate marbles in their original box would sell at auction for $2,000 to $3,000 (or more) each. The above are called cyclones and cobras (the only real difference is in the pattern, so the naming is mostly arbitrary).

Somewhere along the border between Tennessee and Kentucky, we pulled over on a stretch of dirt where a man had set up some tables in front of his recreational vehicle. He was the kind of man whose gentleness made you want to linger longer than normal, hoping to find something to buy. Among the rather middling merchandise, I spotted something pink in a small brown box. Upon closer inspection it looked like a clamshell with a heavy-duty spring. It was only after I pulled the accompanying exercise

manual—featuring June Wilkinson, "famous star of stage and screen, the girl with the world's loveliest bust-line,"—that I realized what it was. It was "The Fabulous Mark Eden Bust Developer," instantly recognizable as a legend of Americana. I couldn't get my money out fast enough.

As I've learned since, from Julie Mangin, the world's largest collector of Mark Eden Bust Developers, Mark Eden was also the creator of Trim Jean inflatable shorts for slimming the hips, the Astro Jogger, and Vacuum pants. Unfortunately, without any medical research, Mark Eden claimed a "scientific breakthrough" and eventually was shut down for mail fraud. But not before selling eighteen thousand Developers at $9.95. Thousands of women spent years mimicking June's eight exercises only to learn her perfection would never be achieved. Nora Ephron, director of *When Harry Met Sally* and *Sleepless in Seattle*, was one of those women and reports that she too found it to fail miserably.

I take Him shopping with me. I say, "OK, Jesus, help me find a bargain."

— Tammy Faye Bakker

Hint: Adorable, cute, and practical . . . before Scotch tape, it would help keep things together.

Answer: string holder

Hint: Helps make a great Southern pie.

Answer: pecan picker upper

Hint: So a traveling salesman didn't get ruffled.

Answer: collapsible clothes hanger

You often learn about and become interested in things you may have never even heard of at garage sales, or encounter some finds that are so unique or just too plain weird that you can't leave them behind. At our next stop I met Dale Howard from Fort Polk, Louisiana. He had a great assortment of items and a sense of humor about his pricing. He priced everything with a ".99" on the end of it, like a discount store, and was also quick to say if I could tell him what he was holding, he'd give me a $1 discount.

I got the item at discount, along with a few other "What is it?"s. Can you guess what they are?

END OF THE ROAD

By the time Sunday rolled around, Bev and I were spent. We had stopped at more than 285 sales (we lost count in Kentucky), talked to hundreds of people, and filled our truck with the results of a lot of wheeling and dealing. I started the trip with $1,000 and a goal to find interesting pieces of Americana and sell the bounty on eBay to see how astute my tastes were. I found fabulous finds, but somewhere between Kentucky and New York, I realized that letting go of them would be a hard, if not impossible, task.

As we drove home, Bev and I relived the stories of our acquisitions. We were able to remember the minutiae of each purchase in astonishing detail, whether it be about the item, the person selling it, or what daydream it had inspired within us. The things we bought grabbed our attention, captured our imagination, and are, in our minds at least, valuable treasures with their own priceless stories.

The rusted Coca-Cola® cooler I bought in Tennessee was once owned by James "Sonny" Francis, a notorious moonshiner from Suck Creek, Tennessee, whose own mother-in-law turned him in. His grandson sold it to me, and according to him, the only way Sonny got out of jail was volunteering as a guinea pig for the flu shot vaccine. I bought that story and the cooler for a hundred bucks. Sonny would be happy to know that it will once again be filled with booze at every summer party.

Are the garden gnomes I bought for $7 "valuable" works of art? Probably not, but the laughs they'll bring are inestimable. The gnomes will deliver precious joy as one by one they start appearing in the yard of my friend, Michelle, known for her resolute bewilderment at why people find them appealing. Nothing says "I'm thinking of you" like a mysterious gnome and a note.

MY $1,000 BOUNTY

collection of metal trays $10

Coca-Cola® cooler $100

wallpaper table $35

fishing lures $31

vintage army supplies $24

metal chairs $20

thirty grocery store signs $15

bar set $12

Jack Daniels opener/spinner $12

vintage ice skating sign $12

homemade flag $3

wooden nativity $12

freezer basket $10

lawn edger $10

Mammy pie bird $10

locker basket $6

mid-century lamp $10

pecan picker upper $10

Mr. Peanut charm bracelet $10

Lloyd Loom child chair $35

Starburst platter and bowl $10

three antique tools $10

three vintage aprons $10

Democratic-party donkey pin $7

garden gnome collection $7

Christmas ornaments $6

three feed sacks $3

tool box $6

art deco vase $5

Bakelite ice cream scoop $5

Civil War knife $5

garden gate $5

barber's pole $320

rooster jewelry box $5

marbles $4

oilcan $4

Christmas decorations $3

early ginger ale opener $3

embroidered tea towel $3

vintage postcards $3

embroidered quilt $60

children's books $2

chrome menu holder $2

clothes hanger $2

lure $2

postcards $2

road reflector $2

Model T brass pump $30

Atlantic City compact $1

beaded placemats $1

bottle topper $1

coin purse $1

comic books $1

World's Fair magnets $3

fondue set $1

Nixon shrinking penny $1

shot set $1

silver broach $2

vintage New York State map $1

wooden dominoes $.75

TOTAL
$933.75

HIDDEN TREASURE

There's hidden treasure out there if you're willing to hunt, track down the prize, and drag it home. Certainly, if you're looking to make money and have a good eye, you can do it by pawing around at garage sales. On eBay, I'd more than double my money on most of the things I bought. (I checked.) Not a bad return. Try doing that in the stock market. But for me, it's not about making money; it's about the adventure, the discovery of something I didn't know, and the creativity it inspires.

If there's one thing I've come to know about garage sales, it's that just when you think you've seen it all, heard it all, and bought it all, some other nice person tacks a sign to a telephone pole and invites you over to poke through her stuff.

It's an invitation that's hard to refuse.

There are, of course, legendary stories of garage sale finds so great they've funded early retirement or so precious they were sent to a museum. We'd all like to land one of those. They are the bejeweled carrots, dangling deliciously before us as a sort of motivating taunt. In June 2005 a woman in Omaha bought a chair at a garage sale. When she got it home, she found $3,000 stuffed inside its cushions. In 1993 Jay and Gail Harley bought a box of yellowed sheet music at a garage sale in Orlando for $2, only to later discover that the lot was from the Civil War and worth thousands of dollars.

Others have found things that have become mysteries to solve. Twenty years after Paul Burks bought an old wooden box covered in leather for $5 at a sale in Philadelphia, he accidentally discovered something tucked inside a hidden compartment. What it is or isn't has inspired much debate, and

TAKE A LOOK AT SALES IN . . . *New Jersey* especially the earliest and latest sales of the year, when the "snowbirds" make their migration south to (or from) their winter homes. As one of the earliest settlements of the British colonies, New Jersey is home to a bounty of antiques, and snowbirds love making "early bird specials."

Would you be able to find the diamond in the rough?

now, after Paul's untimely death, his son, Ashley, has taken up the quest to get to the bottom of what was in the false top of the box.

I looked Ashley up after reading about the item in Alabama's *Montgomery Advertiser*, and called him. "Dad had thrown the box into the back of his truck to take to the dump," Ashley told me. "He was cleaning out his workshop, and when he went back out with another load, he saw the box had broken and something was hidden inside. It was a scroll of paper tied with a piece of gold cord, an empty velvet bag, and a wasp nest." When his father unrolled the paper, what he discovered was an ink-stained copy of the Declaration of Independence.

What he found might not just be any copy but what is known as a Dunlap Broadside, one of the original copies of the Declaration printed on July 4 and 5, 1776, by Philadelphia printer John Dunlap. There's speculation he created anywhere from two hundred to five hundred of the things so that they could be sent out by horseback to the thirteen colonies before colonial leaders met to sign it officially. Historians assume that nervous recipients might have hidden the treasonous sheets immediately upon receipt for fear of being discovered by the British. There are only twenty-five copies in existence.

Ashley Burks's father told his friend Bert Bodiford, a history buff who worked for the sheriff's office, and the two men sought out experts to weigh in on its authenticity. Their hunt yielded more questions than answers. While other copies have the printed name of Continental Congress president John Hancock, the Burks's copy appears to have Hancock's actual signature as well as ink-stained handprints on the back. One expert suggests it could be the first Dunlap broadside printed, and a handwriting expert believes the Hancock signature is real.

But others think it's a cleverly doctored reproduction, and that though the paper appears genuine, it seems artificially aged and was in contact with chemicals that weren't around in the eighteenth century.

"That box was in my dad's shop where he worked on cars," Ashley counters. "Of course there were chemicals in there."

Not to mention that somebody probably sprayed that wasp's nest too.

"Why don't you get it appraised by Sotheby's or take it to one of the museums?" I asked him.

"My dad was told it was too expensive," he said. "And he also didn't like taking it out of the bank vault." Reading between the lines, I realized that some of the "experts" might have been interested in a piece of the action. Not wanting him to think I was one of those, I treaded lightly in my advice, but I did make sure he knew about perhaps the greatest garage sale find ever and its remarkable similarities.

In 1989 a Pennsylvania man bought an old painting at a sale because he liked the frame, only to get home and discover that beneath the painting was a folded 15 $3/4$ x 19 $3/4$" Declaration of Independence behind the canvas. He was so sure it was a reproduction he sat on it for two years. Finally a friend convinced him to have it appraised at Sotheby's. It sold in 1991 for $2.4 million, and nine years later was sold again for $8.1 million during an online auction.

Ashley vows to persist. "It's not about the money," he told me. "I just know my dad would want me to get to the bottom of this."

It is this kind of hopeful mystery that makes for great garage saling lore.

Yes, we all can fantasize about the *Antiques Road Show* moment in which someone tells us the lamp we bought for $4 at a yard sale is a $50,000 piece made by Dirk van Erp, a master of the Arts and Crafts movement. (It happened.) Or dream of discovering an original copy of the Declaration of Independence hidden beneath the false top of an old box, like the one sitting guardedly in an Alabama bank vault. Moments like that are like winning the lottery. But, hey, you never know. There's always next weekend....

PART II
DESIGN

When I first bought my house in upstate New York, I was on one of my rental-car escapes from Manhattan. I stopped at a realty office in the Catskills and asked to see some houses. I bought the first house I was shown, and, truth be told, the first house I had ever looked at. I had no intention of actually buying a house—I was just escaping the city.

Edgewater Farm, built in 1924, sits on a trout stream and was a bungalow colony—a place where, from the thirties to the late fifties, New Yorkers came to escape city life with a summer stay in the country,

for a week, a month, or for the season. For over three decades, each year from Memorial Day to Labor Day, eighty people were served breakfast, lunch, and dinner in the farmhouse. They'd spend nights living "cottage cool" in one of the bungalows along the stream, and Saturday nights in the Rec Hall, performing skits, playing games, and dancing. Think *Dirty Dancing* creekside.

I was sold instantly. I had a country house. A mortgage. And not a stitch of furniture. I did what came naturally. I had an empty house, so I went garage saling.

I discovered the Catskills is home to very satisfying yard sale shopping and to some terrific dealers, who scour yard sales with keen eyes and impeccable taste and put it all together in a unique way. On my first garage sale weekend out, I met Bev when I stopped in her store Cathouse Antiques, housed in the garage adjacent to her gingerbread Victorian house. I was hooked on Bev and her treasure trove of twentieth-century beauties the day we met.

"Is the Madame here?" I asked.

"You've found her," she replied.

I had my eye on a Hoosier-style cabinet I saw in her window. A thirties-era Napanee Electrified Kitchenette, in perfect condition—the inside panels inscribed with measurement conversions, "household hints," and "things worth knowing." It was waiting for me.

I calmly walked toward the Cathouse Madame's perch. Looking not the least bit interested, I casually glanced at a lamp, lifted the lid of a pink canister, and rang an old cowbell. . . . Then, I caught her off guard: "What kind of deal could you give me on the Kitchenette?"

"Hmmmm," she purred.

Do's and Don'ts for Buyers

Do

- Go early for the best stuff, late for the best bargains.

- Pack a tape measure, something to wrap breakables, and a bottle of water.

- Park appropriately (not in the flower bed or the neighbor's yard).

- Head back to your car if you pass people walking away from a garage sale empty-handed.

- Ignore the dust and dirt. Beauty is more than surface deep.

- Think about repurposing old items.

- Pick it up if you're interested in it. If it's still on the table, it's still fair game.

- Ask questions.

- Buy it if you like it or if it reminds you of someone you like.

- Ask "What's your best price?" followed by "How much if I buy all this stuff?"

- Ask other buyers if they've been to other good sales and share what you know.

- Realize that fancier neighborhoods have fancier stuff.

- Keep moving. You can't see everything, and you want to hit as many sales as you can.

Don't

- Be pushy.

- Call your friend to check eBay or book values.

- Buy it just because it's cheap.

- Buy things that need fixing, unless you're really going to fix them.

- Buy things that might be dangerous to you or someone you love.

- Buy damaged goods if you're going to resell.

- Assume that all the pieces are there in an opened five-hundred-piece puzzle.

- Be guaranteed that something is "authentic," unless you're an expert.

- Ask to use their bathroom.

- Nickel and dime. If something is a nickel, don't offer a penny.

- Try to return something after you've driven off with it.

- Wear expensive shoes. Sellers often judge how much you'll pay by the clothes you're wearing. The finer the stitch, the higher the price.

Did I sound too desperate? Could she see through my veneer? She pulled out her calculator, did some figuring, wrote a number on a torn piece of brown paper, and slid it across the counter to me. I slowly lifted her proposal as if it were the last slip in a who-gets-in-the-lifeboat

competition. I picked up the slip of paper, looked at it, realized it was upside down, flipped it right side up, and proclaimed, "Sold."

As we celebrated our deal, Bev told me to read the placards inside the cabinet. Household hints—"To remove fruit stains, pour boiling water over stained surface having it fall from a distance of three feet." It sounded tricky. "For a burn, apply equal parts of white of egg and olive oil mixed together and then cover with a piece of old linen." Then, the most important addendum to the cure-a-burn directions: "If applied at once, no blister will form."

Ouch. For burns, you might need to plan ahead.

PERFECTLY IMPERFECT

Garage saling proves that life can be perfect in its imperfections. Having nice things doesn't have to be expensive, and spotting the potential in something that others are done with brings great satisfaction. To show you what I mean, here's a tour of Edgewater Farm. Maybe you'll get some ideas or get inspired on how to incorporate garage sale finds into your life with your own cast-off style.

This cookie jar is a great example of a shelf piece. It's chipped and without a lid, but sitting up on a shelf it sure brings a smile.

An enamel drainboard kitchen sink that was $20. A toolbox utensil holder that I bought for $7.

KITCHEN

Using the Napanee Kitchenette as my centerpiece, I designed my kitchen around it, finding things that complemented the look. I bought a service for eight of Royal China's Starburst dinnerware for $10 at a garage sale and was thrilled to see that my dishes were available on eBay. New to eBay, I placed a bid. And then I found more—and placed five more bids. I now adore eBay. It is a 24/7/365 garage sale, and, for me, a perfect distraction anytime. But then I was unaware of how eBay worked. By the following week, I had five e-mails congratulating me on being the highest bidder on Star Glow dishes. I can now serve dinner for fifty.

The enamel-top table and chairs were bought for $150. A vintage "champagne" bucket was $3. And last but not least, Swanky Swigs that were $4 each are great for champagne and wine.

The vintage toaster, blender, and other appliances work better than new and were each less than $10. The "island" is an old table with great patina ($4) topped with a baker's rack for chopping.

LIVING ROOM

My living room is about cocktail parties—designed specifically for friends and me to have a good time. There's no plastic on the furniture here; everything is meant to be used and make us cozy. My decorating philosphy is living should be comfortable and fun. The heart of the room is a 1904 Lipton's Coffee shipping box filled with my vintage board game collection, including Risk, Parcheesi, Password, $20,000 Pyramid, All in the Family, Twister, and a raucous Richard Dawson version of Family Feud.

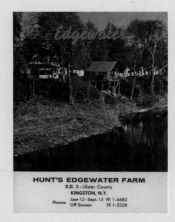

In the top drawer of a dresser at a garage sale I found some old advertising brochures from the fifties inviting people for a summer stay in my cottages. They are an important historic part of the living room.

ABOVE: Old boxes make the perfect container for a rotation of seasonal plants. This painted one was $2. LEFT: The vintage store postcard holder with old postcards was $10. Old benches are versatile and always useful, either for seating or display; this one was $15.

Here's an antique Mexican desk that I bought at Tom Foolery's barn sale for $100. Someone offered double the money while I went to get a truck. Fortunately, Tom is honest.

The dining room is built around a barn door table, which I put together for less than $125. The barn door came, appropriately, from a barn sale. I was intrigued by the width of one of the boards, which is over eighteen inches wide.

DINING ROOM

"Formal" dining rooms don't have to be stuffy. The pastiche of patinas in my dining room pays tribute to history and tells guests that something has probably been spilled here before. I don't cook too often, but no matter what is on the menu, I'm not scared to use the "good dishes." I want guests to know they are special.

ABOVE: My dishes are Franciscan Pottery Starburst—manufactured from 1954-1957 by Gladding, McBean & Company—and are one of my most cherished family heirlooms. As many women did in the fifties, my grandmother and her friend Reba bought their pieces from the "fancy" jewelry store. The serving pieces are hard to find (and typically expensive), but I've gotten lucky at several garage sales.

RIGHT: Pie safes traditionally were made to keep the pies safe from critters while they cooled. Since I'm more of a bartender than pastry chef, my pie safe serves as a liquor cabinet. It cost $50.

BATH

Bathrooms are the great escape mini-environments that should evoke calm. In each bathroom, I've kept the vintage feel using finds that are unique and affordable. Wall treatments don't have to be expensive. I wove ⅛" painted plywood for the walls downstairs and used sheetrock mud to give the upstairs bath a French plaster look. But I must admit, I learned my lessons with plumbing: new is certainly more efficient than old.

The antique pedestal sink was a great find for $60, but it's a constant battle to keep the faucets from springing a leak. On my list is finding suitable reproductions. I found the white subway tile for $15 at a tag sale. Someone's unfinished project is my gain.

ABOVE: Old lights are a great find as long as you're willing to take the time to rewire. I've been lucky to find authentic fixtures that suit my house.

LEFT: Peeling paint can be beautiful. I used a wire brush to scrape off loose paint from this $5 find, then sealed it with a light coat of polyurethane spray. The barbershop jars were $30 for the set and make the perfect holders for bathroom accoutrements. The shutters are one of my chance finds. I bought them at a barn sale for $5, not having my window measurements with me. I got them home to find that they were the perfect fit. All they needed was a quick coat of paint and some screws.

That man is the richest whose pleasures are the cheapest.

– Henry David Thoreau, journal, March 11, 1856

BEDROOM

After many years needing window treatments, I found the perfect solution by accident. I bought a vintage Nystrom roll-up school map of Europe at the World's Largest Garage Sale in Warrensburg, New York, for $5, only to get home and realize it was the exact measurement for the bedroom windows. The most educational shade!

LEFT: I've repurposed this potato/onion holder: The bottom is ideal for magazines and vitamins; the top stores jewelry. It was $3. My Resolute woodstove by Vermont Castings (not shown) was $50; romantic nights and oil bill savings are an added bonus.

RIGHT: For the matching pair of windows across the room, I lucked into finding its United States twin brother the following week when I went to Zaborski Emporium. After telling owner Stan Zaborski the story of how I was going to use it, he gave it to me as a gift because I "realize they're priceless." That's the luck of garage saling.

STUDY

The study is a versatile room used for reading, napping, and playing games. I wanted to give it a proper feel without being stuffy and achieved it with a few garage sale finds that say fun.

ABOVE: This antique English bowling game was one of the more expensive purchases in my house, but was given to me as a gift by my friend Barbara Corcoran when our book, *Use What You've Got*, made the best-seller list. Each pin is hand-carved and the alley is inlaid. Knowing I love games, she says she knew I had to have it when she spotted it at an auction.

RIGHT: I love the colors on this abacus, and though I have no idea how to count on it, I did figure that $25 for a piece of functional art seemed like a good buy.

LEFT: The inlaid drop-leaf table can be used as a desk or for a raucous board game when the leaf is opened. I've been told by antiques dealers it's worth much more than the $75 I paid for it. Antique children's toys are very collectible, and it isn't uncommon for unique toys from the nineteenth century to go for thousands of dollars. I found this adorable giraffe for $20.

ABOVE: Every farmhouse needs a milking pitcher. I rotate greenery and flowers at different times of the year in this $7 find.

PORCH

The life of the house begins on the porch. I put a porch back on the house, then added to it the things they would have had in the forties and fifties.

RIGHT: The porch swing has character and looks like it has always been there. Besides, "new" on my porch would have looked downright out of place. The swing was $20. Wagons make the perfect coffee tables. They are easily moved to where they are needed, and can be fancy or casual. I've gotten several of them over the years, ranging in price from $5 for a junker to $75 for a good-condition Radio Flyer, and use them in various ways all around my property.

BELOW: Metal rockers like these aren't impossible to find, but finding them in good condition is difficult. If you're buying vintage and it's metal, make sure the joints aren't rusted through.

GARDEN

Gardening is the secret path to a happy home. Whether it's one carefully cared for geranium or a giant perennial bed, putting your hands in soil keeps you grounded, and taking care of something keeps you alive. I love to spend mornings in the garden, weeding, pruning, and cutting my flowers, then taking an armful and arranging them in great (read: cheaply acquired and unique) bottles and containers all over the house. And, yes, I've even bought plants at a yard sale!

ABOVE: You didn't notice the heads were broken off the handles of this urn, right? See how this imperfection doesn't matter? It was an "archeological discovery" at $25.

RIGHT: These old lifeguard chairs make the perfect garden seating for $75. The white table was found in a "free" pile and repainted.
LEFT: This garden cart worked then, and it works now. Old bottles usually range in price from 25¢ to $1, unless they're collectible. Then you'll need money, not flowers.

The barber's chair was my first find for the space. It cost $75 and took three men to move, but gave me an instant theme for the space. The dentist's chair was even cheaper but was also a bear to move. The dentist's office side table was a painless purchase for $12.

This table from a gynecologist's office was $50, and though it sometimes makes my women friends look twice, it's functional and always gets a laugh. The old record player works well and was a find at $10, and it allows me to buy well-priced records that catch my eye. This one is bawdy and well worth the $3.

CLUBHOUSE

When Edgewater Farm was operating as a bungalow colony, this building is where the workers slept and was appropriately deemed "The Seldom Inn." Using garage sale finds I turned it into a little clubhouse for friends who smoke. They love it, and I don't have to feel guilty when I remind them to take their habit outside the main house.

The croquet set was $20 and is great fun in the summer. At the same yard sale, I also bought a shuffleboard set and plan to paint a shuffleboard court on the floor of the recreation hall. The other elements were each less than $5 and are all at hand to bring about a good time outdoors.

RECREATION HALL

The recreation hall was once the Saturday nightspot for dancing, bingo, and talent shows. I use it as a party space and have several talented friends who perform inside to standing room only crowds. Wanting to keep the vintage feel, I highlighted the age rather than covering it up, and invested some money to reinforce the structural integrity.

TOP, RIGHT: The barber's pole was my "World's Longest Yard Sale" splurge at $320, but I always wanted one and knew the color and feel would be just right for the hall's porch. I've acquired the signs from $5 to $20 each at various sales. Signage with great graphics or colors is highly collectible. The chalkboard announces events and welcomes guests to Edgewater Farm. It was a deal at $3. The rockers are from the historic Mohonk Mountain House. They are very comfortable and, at $75 for the pair, were cheaper than new.

TOP, NEAR RIGHT: The ceiling is old roof metal from a barn that I bought for $120. I love the color and the texture. The vintage ceiling fan was $20, but had to be rewired.

TOP, FAR RIGHT: The chandelier was $30. Notice how it accommodates candles as well.

BOTTOM, NEAR RIGHT: The recreation hall houses a few things I've saved for the future, including toboggans I bought for $25, which I'll mount on the wall and use as a great set of shelves for my dishes.

BOTTOM, FAR RIGHT: The phone booth was $40 and is the best place for people at dinner parties to take cell phone calls.

THE GUEST ROOM

My favorite room and perhaps the most important room in any house—the guest room—is where we welcome special friends and tuck them into their home away from home. As in the kitchen with the Napanee Kitchenette, something as simple as a trunk inspired the design of this room and helped recreate the joy of thirty summers, the fun of a thousand kids.

The camp trunk I bought from Bev for $75 (Cleon Moore, a boy nicknamed Butch, owned it at one time) is one of my most cherished pieces. The trunk inspired the room and helped bring the décor together, but it's more than that. This is a room for the kid I don't have—or for the kid I'm trying never to forget. Who knows, maybe one day there will be a little kid running around this room playing with all these things I've collected. Until then, I get to enjoy the fun Cleon Moore's trunk has brought to Edgewater Farm, and the memories he unknowingly inspired. The kid nicknamed Butch who took his blue trunk to summer camp in the Catskills, played by the creek, and did shows on Saturday night. That's him. The kid that had the time of his life.

RIGHT: This old school song strip from the early twentieth century features the tune "The Spider and the Fly." The metal army bed was $10—with delivery! It was one of my earliest barn sale purchases. I stripped it, sanded it, and polyurethaned it to prevent rusting. It has old-fashioned bedsprings, and guests love it. Atop the doctor's office side table I purchased for $45 is a vintage children's Indian lamp with a teepee base that was $15.

And so, it happens like that. One sale at a time—one room at a time—a style, a look, a home comes together, giving us a sense of place, bringing comfort, and making us happy. That's the lifestyle we all want. There's no excuse to live with a room you don't like when all it takes to bring it to life is some creative thinking, a few bucks, and a Saturday cruise around town. Imagination is free, and yard sale shopping is cheap.

Get out there and hunt for your treasure!

LET'S GO SALING!: GARAGE SALE GUIDE

Garage sales have long been known as a great way to spend a Saturday, but with the explosion in popularity, they are now a trendy, mainstream obsession. Here's a comprehensive look at the best of the biggest. I've met many people at these that are on "garage sale vacations" and having the time of their lives. It's fun, it's cheap, it's family friendly, and you return home with the best souvenirs.

Most sales are loosely organized, though some have official maps of sites. You might go from bumper to bumper to traveling miles with great scenery but no sales. Consult Garagesaleamerica.com for this year's specific dates and links to resources and further information.

APRIL

ANTIQUE ALLEY & YARD SALE. Started in 1999, it spans fifteen miles through central Texas, from Cleburne to Grandview on FM 4 (what was originally called a state farm-to-market road). Expect  to see five hundred vendors from several states offering antiques, collectibles, arts, crafts, food, yard sale items, and more; also held each year in September. For more information, check the website: http://alley.cleburne.com.

WORLD'S LARGEST YARD SALE. Established in 1998, this community event is set up on Main Street in Rock Hill, South Carolina. It has competitors who'll argue the "world's largest" title, but, regardless of wordplay,  this event features over two hundred booths and countless treasures. To heighten the frenzy, gates to "the yard" open at 8:00 A.M. and not a minute sooner. For more information, check the website: www.heraldyardsale.com.

MAY

100-MILE GARAGE SALE. This sale has existed since 1993. It spans one hundred miles on the Wisconsin and Minnesota sides of the Mississippi River from Alma, Wisconsin, to Bay City, Wisconsin, on Wisconsin 35, and Red Wing, Minnesota, to Winona, Minnesota, on U.S. 61. The Mississippi Great Road was listed among the top three scenic drives in America. A trail of distinctive colored ribbons identifies participating garage sales. This event is rain or shine! For more information, check the website: www.mississippi-river.org.

100-MILE YARD SALE. Since 1999 this yard sale has spanned one hundred miles in southeast Missouri from Jackson to Kennett on Missouri 25. It is held every Memorial Day Weekend, from Thursday to Monday. For more information, check the website: www.jacksonmo.com (click on events calendar under "Tourism").

GREAT U.S. 50 YARD SALE. Started in 2000, the sale spans 3,073 miles—from Ocean City, Maryland, to Sacramento, California, on U.S. 50. The sale crosses mountains and deserts, as well as farmland. The official yard sale takes place over three days; there are no set hours. For more information, check the website: www.route50.com/yardsale.html.

HISTORICAL NATIONAL ROAD YARD SALE DAYS. Established

in 2003, the sale spans 824 miles from Baltimore, Maryland, to St. Louis, Missouri, on historic U.S. 40, also known as the National Road (the road is two hundred years old). Traffic is often bumper to bumper, and parking spaces and restaurant tables are at a premium. For more information, check the website: www.oldstorefrontantiques.com.

JUNE

13+ MILES OF YARD SALE EXTRAVAGANZA. This sale, established in 2003, spans more than seventy miles through southern Washington State from Lyle to Klickitat and Goldendale on State Route 142, to Wishram on U.S. 97 on State Route 14, and back to Lyle on 14 with offshoots at Dallesport. The name comes from the distance between Lyle and Klickitat (the first sale's distance). Lyle is renowned for being one of the best areas in the United States for windsurfing, fishing, hiking, and boating. It's one of the smallest towns in America, with the following population (as of 2000): 530 (males: 265, females: 265). Wishram's claim to fame is that explorers Lewis and Clark traveled this area extensively, and wrote about their experiences. For more information, check the website: www.goldendalechamber.org (click on "Event" calendar).

DIXIE HIGHWAY YARD SALE. Held the first weekend of June along "the granddaddy of Interstate 75," Georgia's first interstate highway. The ninety-mile trip is filled with sites and good food. Make a stop at Doug's Place Restaurant in Emerson for fried chicken and catfish inside an original Dixie Highway gas station. For more information, check the website: www.dixiehighway.org.

HIGHWAY 6 GARAGE SALE. Established in 1999, this sale spans two hundred miles across northern Missouri from St. Joseph to Hannibal on Missouri 6 north of U.S. 36. St. Joseph is a unique community famous for its

historical link to the Pony Express and Jesse James, and for its many museums. Hannibal, Missouri, is the hometown of Mark Twain, and his childhood house is still the area's most popular tourist attraction. For more information, check the website www.jamesportmo.com.

HIGHWAY 68/80 400-MILE ANTIQUES, COLLECTIBLES, AND STUFF SALE. Started in 2004, this sale spans four hundred miles across Kentucky from Paducah to Maysville on U.S. 68, which also shares the route with Kentucky 80 part of the way. Sixty communities participate in this annual four-day event the first weekend in June. For more information, check the website: www.10000trails.com/hwy68-80/sale.

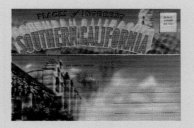

ROUTE 66 GARAGE SALE. This sale spans about four hundred miles along "America's Main Street," Oklahoma's historic Route 66—which now has different route numbers depending on where you are—from Quapaw to Texola. Historic U.S. 66, also known as the Mother Road, went from Chicago to Los Angeles. There are many quaint and wonderful small towns and big cities with their wild mix of art deco and modern architectural styles. For more information, check the website: www.oklahomaroute66.com (click on calendar).

JULY

100-MILE YARD SALE. Started in 1998, this sale spans one hundred miles through central Pennsylvania's Clearfield, Elk ,and Cameron counties in a route from Shawville to Karthaus on Pennslvania 879, through the Quehanna Wild Area to Medix Run on Quehanna Highway with an offshoot to Pottersdale, to

Driftwood on Pennsylvania 555, to Sinemahoning on Pennsylvania 120, and to Wykoff Run back to Quehanna Highway. For more information, check the website: www.visitclearfieldcounty.org (click on large calendar).

FIFTY-MILE GARAGE SALE ON ROUTE 90. Since 1988 this sale has spanned fifty miles through upstate New York on NY 90 from Montezuma to Homer. For more information, check the website: www.tourcayuga.com.

FOURTH OF JULY 52-MILE YARD SALE. Since 2005 this sale has spanned fifty-two miles through eastern Kentucky from Irvine to Jackson on Kentucky 52. This is another classic small town, with a population of 1,131; it is home to the annual Wooly Worm Festival! For more information, check the website: www.beattyville.org.

AUGUST

ANTIQUE YARD SALE TRAIL. Since 2003 this yard sale has spanned more than two hundred miles through eastern Michigan from Sebewaing to New Baltimore on Michigan 25 and 29, which hugs the waters of Lake Huron, the St. Clair River, and Lake St. Clair. For more information, check the website: www.yardsaletrail.com.

BARGAINS GALORE ON 64. Since 2000 this sale has spanned 160 miles through Arkansas from Fort Smith to Beebe on U.S. 64. It was designated a "travel treasure" by *Southern*

Traveler magazine for its friendly atmosphere and the beautiful vistas. For more information, check the website: www.bargainsgaloreon64.com.

HIGHWAY 127 CORRIDOR SALE. Since 1987 this has been the World's Longest Yard Sale, spanning 450 miles from Covington, Kentucky, to Gadsden, Alabama, on U.S. 127. This one's the granddaddy of multistate yard sales. For more information, check the website: www.127sale.com.

HIGHWAY 141 GARAGE SALE. Established in 2003, this sale spans eighty miles in west central Iowa from Manilla to Granger on Iowa 141. For more information, check the website: www.141sale.com.

LINCOLN HIGHWAY BUY-WAY YARD SALE. Started in 2005, this sale spans more than four hundred miles from Fort Wayne, Indiana, to East Liverpool, Ohio. Lincoln Highway was the first paved route from New York to San Francisco. In Ohio and eastern Indiana it generally follows U.S. 30. For more information, check the website: www.historicbyway.com.

U.S. 12 HERITAGE TRAIL SALE. Established in 2003, this sale spans 212 miles through Michigan from New Buffalo to Detroit on U.S. 12, also called the Old Sauk Trail. The trail actually started some ten thousand years ago when it was the longest Mastodon travelway, and it is still the longest ever found according to paleontologists. For more information, check the website: www.swmicomm.org/SWMC/US12.htm (go to "Events").

SEPTEMBER

BENTON COUNTY BARGAIN HIGHWAY. This sale, started in 1998, spans thirty miles through West Tennessee's Benton County, from U.S. 641

at Interstate 40 to Tennessee 192; it goes through Holladay and Camden, and Big Sandy on Tennessee 69A. For more information, check the website: www.benton-countycamden.com/tourism/events.html.

EAST 80 YARD SALE. Established in 2000, this sale spans fifty-five miles through eastern Kentucky on Kentucky 80 from Somerset to Manchester. For more information, check the website: www.east80yardsale.cjb.net.

HIGHWAY 75 MARKETPLACE. Established in 2003, this sale spans four hundred miles through western Minnesota from Luverne to Hallock on U.S. 75, also known as the King of Trails. For more information, check the website: www.highway75.com.

LABOR DAY 25-MILE YARD SALE. This sale, started in 2001, spans twenty-five miles in southeast Missouri from U.S. 60 around Wappapello Lake on Missouri Highway T. For more information, check the website: www.fishermansnet.net.

LAKE WEST CHAMBER OF COMMERCE 25-MILE GARAGE SALE. Since 2002 this sale has spanned twenty-five miles in central Missouri from Gravois Mills to the Greenview area west of Lake of the Ozarks on Missouri 5 north of U.S. 54. For more information, check the website: www.lakewestchamber.com.

OCTOBER

HIGHWAY 411 YARD SALE. Started in 2003 this sale spans almost four hundred miles from Leeds, Alabama, through Georgia to Newport, Tennessee, on U.S. 411. For more information, check the website: www.hwy411yardsale.com.

HI-WAY 80 SALE. Since 2002, it spans 374 miles from East Texas to Vicksburg, Mississippi, on historic U.S. 80, which winds around Interstate 20. For more information, check the website: www.us80.com.

ROLLER COASTER FAIR & YARD SALE. This sale, established in 1986, spans 150 miles from Mammoth Cave, Kentucky, through Tennessee around Dale Hollow Lake and back to Glasgow, Kentucky, on  Kentucky routes 70, 90, 63, and 163; Tennessee 51, 52, and 111; U.S. 127; and Kentucky 90. The first part of the route ending in Byrdstown, Tennessee, is historic Cordell Hull Highway, built in 1805 and named in 1935 to honor President Franklin D. Roosevelt's secretary of state. (There is no actual roller coaster.) For more information, check the website: www.rollercoasterfair.com.

WARRENSBURG GARAGE SALE. The World's Largest Garage Sale was established in 1979. It spans about ten miles in upstate New York from St. George to north of Warrensburg into the Adirondacks on U.S. 9, expanding from a citywide sale in Warrensburg. For more information, check the website: www.warrensburggaragesale.com.

GARAGE SALE GLOSSARY

Garage sales operate in a parallel universe, with a language all their own.
Here's a guide to help you wheel and deal with the best of them.

"A Find"
Treasures don't get any better.

Antique
A collectible, decorative, or household object valued because of its age; typically items more than one hundred years old.

As is
When you hand over the cash, the object is yours with every chip, ding, and crack.

Bargain
Something you didn't know you needed at a price you couldn't resist.

Bargaining
A sport in which buyer and seller engage in a give-and-take to arrive at a mutually satisfactory price for merchandise without arriving at blows.

Barn sale
A delightful garage sale shopping experience within a large outbuilding, often on a farm, in which the owner has rustled up some big pieces, benches, gates, and farmhouse kitchen sinks, as well as an array of tools, signs, jars, and assorted treasures.

Bid box
At some estate/tag sales, rather than paying the asking price of more expensive items on the first day, you may be able to put a bid in. (Hint: if you want better chances of winning the item, bid higher than 50 percent and add some change; for example, if the asking price is $100, offer more than half and round up a little, say to $63.74).

Bloomin' onion
2,130 calories of deep-fried-onion delight, generally served at flea markets and "event" garage sales.

Bluffing
Pretending to be only vaguely interested in an item in order to score a better price.

Boardinghouse reach
When your arm extends two feet from its socket and over someone else in order to reach across a table and grab something delicious.

Book value
Value of a collectible or antique item in a reference book; often referenced to point out appropriate pricing by a seller.

Box lot
Any number of items thrown in a box that you pay one price for, bought in hopes that amidst the burnt pot holders, Tupperware, and a couple of trashy paperbacks, a treasured prize awaits.

Bragging piece
An incredible piece scored for an incredible price.

Car boot sale
England's answer to a garage sale, named such—it means selling out of the car trunk—by Barry Peverett in 1980.

Caveat emptor
"Let the buyer beware" and take responsibility for the condition of the items he purchases, which should be examined before purchase.

Cheese fries
3,010 calories of artery-clogging delight, generally available at flea markets and "event" garage sales; see also bloomin' onion and elephant ear.

Chin stroker
An indecisive buyer.

Chip
A nick out of pottery in which the rough interior can be felt.

Collectibles
Beauty is often in the eye of the beholder.

Collector
The beholder.

Crazing
Also known as "alligatoring," this is a crackled surface effect within the glazes of pottery, not a crack.

Dicker
To bargain.

Disposophobia
The fear of getting rid of stuff, no matter how worthless or how valuable.

"Don't know if it works"
(It doesn't.)

Drive-bys
Slowing down enough to glance at the offerings before hitting the pedal, not so subtly indicating, "your stuff stinks."

Early birds
Shoppers who come ready for coffee and bagels prior to the start of a sale.

Elephant ears
Fried dough sprinkled with confectioners' sugar, a forty-four-gram-of-fat delight often served at "event" garage sales and flea markets (also known as "funnel cakes"); see also bloomin' onion and cheese fries.

Estate sale
A sale usually pertaining to all contents in a home, often indicating the owner has passed away or moved into a retirement home.

"Everything must go!"
Often this means it must go right to the dump!

Fanny pack
Money-pouch choice of most shoppers, it holds money, keys, and other essentials, enabling two free hands to tote the treasures.

Female sale
Anthropologist Gretchen M. Herrmann's observation that sales hosted by women are often stereotypically neater and more organized than those of men, generally featuring clean, priced, and well-displayed items and a hostess who is prepared with plenty of change.

Fleabite
A tiny chip in pottery or glass, usually not large enough to warrant foregoing a purchase.

Flea market
A place where vendors come to sell their wares, usually inexpensive items that range

from Made in China new to antique old.

Foxing
The irregular spotting or rusting of printed material.

Garage sale
An informal, irregularly scheduled (read: not required to get permits or pay sales tax) homegrown marketplace of unwanted items from the home.

Gawkers
Those who attend sales as voyeurs, not buyers.

"Good stuff"
Often used in classifieds and on signs; hit-or-miss on whether true or not.

Haggling
Remember: negotiating is friendly; haggling seems insulting.

HTF
Hard to find.

Jelly Jar Sale
A couple of tables with piles of trashy trinkets on them, a surefire way to waste time on both the seller's and buyer's part.

Junk
Item that has lost its value to the owner and can be sold to some lucky new owner.

Junque
"Junk" in disguise. Don't be fooled.

"Kiss & kick"
A technique of bargaining in which an item is admired and respected, followed by a pointing out of its dramatic flaw: "I love your Hull vase. How'd it get chipped?"

Kitsch
Something enjoyable for its retro value or unintentional, ironic humor or garishness; lawn ornaments and garden gnomes are examples.

Lurkers
Those who attend garage sales with no intention of making a purchase.

Male sale
Characterized by anthropologist Gretchen M. Herrmann as "chaos on the lawn," it often includes unpriced merchandise like cassettes, old tools, and jumbled clothes in decaying boxes.

MIB
"Mint in (original) box."

MIJ
Made in Japan.

Mint
In perfect condition.

Museum sale
People who indicate with their high prices that they obviously don't want to sell their stuff, they just want you to ogle it.

NBW
Never been worn.

Patina
Derived from years of use, this effect gives a piece character; includes flaking paint, nicks, crackling, and wear that can only be derived from age.

Pickers
Professional shoppers who buy and resell to antique dealers or thrift shops; also known as "the middleman."

Price realized
The price that is actually obtained by a seller for an object.

Repro

Reproduction of a collectible, often so good it can even fool an expert; see caveat emptor.

Repurposing

To use or convert for use in another format or product.

Roadkill

Removing enough of a desired object to make it worthless to others who might come along before you have the chance to haul it away; for example, removing the drawers from a heavy dresser that won't fit in the car.

Robin Hood sale

A sale in a wealthy neighborhood that makes for a lot of Merry Men and Women.

Shelf piece

Something that is not quite perfect but looks great on a shelf anyway.

Skunked

Not finding a sale, or worse, finding a sale that has nothing but smelly finds.

Sniper

A last-minute bidder or buyer, who swoops in at the last seconds of an auction or sale and outbids the competition; often used as a strategy on eBay.

Squatter

Vendor who sets up in a highly trafficked area they don't own.

Sticker price

Remember: the asking price on a garage sale item is not necessarily the final price.

Stoop sale

A sale in urban areas.

Tag sale

Denotes a better level of merchandise priced to move and generally finds bigger pieces (often in their natural habitat).

Tchotchkes

Derived from the Slavic word for toys, it's often a trinket or little knickknack that brings joy.

"The lot"

Buying everything of a kind.

Tire kicking

Testing things out, plugging things in.

Value

The fair price of an item to both buyer and seller.

Verdigris

The attractive pale blue-green of aged copper, which protects it from the elements.

Vultures

Worse than early birds, these predators will show up at a garage sale before any lights are on in the house and peer in the windows.

Yard sale

A garage sale without the garage.

Yellowing

A uniform color change of paper, typically indicative of poor paper quality; it degrades the value of printed materials.

ACKNOWLEDGMENTS

This book wouldn't be possible (and my house would be empty) if not for all those who woke up early on Saturday mornings and let me snoop through their stuff. Thanks for the treasures. Except for the Longaberger two-pie basket, they are all doing fine and the stories of their provenance are legendary.

To my friends in Ulster County: thank you for the happy adventure, especially Michelle Lay and Beverly Saponaro who pointed me to the good stuff. To the Sensationals, thanks for helping me stay sane. Sort of. I cherish the fun. I salute the Hunt family for creating "Edgewater Farm" and throw a big kiss to Cenaida Johannis who helps me keep it together. And to Mary and Tim Cleary, my life wouldn't be the same if you hadn't helped me plant a garden. I am blessed to know you.

To my family who celebrated my quirkiness and humored my pursuit of big dreams, I send you love from New York. Jenny Mitchell, thanks for loving a good story and good finds as much as me. And to my brother Brian, I apologize for not grabbing Bert & Ernie in Georgia. It's the one that got away.

To Barbara Corcoran, friend and confidante, thanks for being you. Here's to our two Scotts (Durkin and Stewart) for introducing us.

Cal Crary, photographer, friend, and Polaroid King, thanks for capturing garage sale magic on film so perfectly. And to Rochelle Riservato, thanks for always coming through.

To my Garage Sale America TV team: Mark Greene, Anne Barliant, Jason Martin, Jeff Gautier, and Ian Lane, your creativity is inspiring.

My agent Todd Shuster at Zachary Shuster Harmsworth is a gem and a gentleman, and my attorney Eric Brown is the kindest pit bull in New York. A special salute to publicist Sy Presten, whose typewriter is well-connected and whose wit is keen.

At HarperCollins, my heartfelt thanks to Marta Schooler and Joe Tessitore, the Good Shepherds, for believing and shaping, and to Gretchen Crary, who in Gawker's taxonomy of publicists is "one in a million." The artistry of Ilana Anger and Kay Schuckhart is on every page; Margarita Vaisman and Dinah Fried kept everything going; and the book wouldn't be in your hands if not for George Bick and the enthusiastic sales force. And to my editor, Liz Sullivan, the Virgo with the great snow globe collection, ever thanks for your attention to detail. It's refreshing and invigorating. (*Psst* . . . for the story she wouldn't let me put in the book, go to Garagesaleamerica.com. Life is a happy compromise.)

And, most of all, love to Scott and Westminster for making life a real treat.